A Heart on Fire

A Heart on Fire

Living as a mystic in today's world

Annika Spalde

Translated by Susan Beard

WILD GOOSE PUBLICATIONS

English edition first published 2010

Wild Goose Publications
4th Floor, Savoy House, 140 Sauchiehall Street, Glasgow G2 3DH, UK
www.ionabooks.com
Wild Goose Publications is the publishing division of the Iona Community.
Scottish Charity No. SC003794. Limited Company Reg. No. SC096243.

ISBN 978-1-905010-68-4

Cover design © Wild Goose Publications

The publishers gratefully acknowledge the support of the Drummond Trust,
3 Pitt Terrace, Stirling FK8 2EY in producing this book.

A catalogue record for this book is available from the British Library.

Overseas distribution:
Australia: Willow Connection Pty Ltd, Unit 4A, 3-9 Kenneth Road,
Manly Vale, NSW 2093
New Zealand: Pleroma, Higginson Street, Otane 4170, Central Hawkes Bay
Canada: Novalis/Bayard Publishing & Distribution, 10 Lower Spadina Ave.,
Suite 400, Toronto, Ontario M5V 2Z2

Printed by Bell & Bain, Thornliebank, Glasgow

Mixed Sources
Product group from well-managed
forests and other controlled sources
www.fsc.org Cert no. TT-COC-002769
© 1996 Forest Stewardship Council

Contents

'Heaven was opened and a fiery light of exceeding brilliance came and permeated my entire brain, inflaming my whole heart and my whole breast, not as in a burning flame but as a flame which warms, like the sun warms anything its rays touch.'

Hildegard of Bingen[1]

Foreword

I have been a Christian ever since I discovered God at a confirmation camp in the summer of 1983 and I have been engaged in global issues ever since I witnessed the poverty in Latin America in 1986. Through the years my faith and commitment have inspired each other in my everyday life and in many different circumstances, such as campaigning against nuclear weapons and the arms trade in the European peace movement, working and living with the homeless while staying in Christian communities in Sweden and the United States, and as a deacon in the suburbs of Gothenburg in Sweden, where I have become involved in religious dialogue. I have often experienced it as a constant stream, an outpouring I consciously seek; a Something – a Someone – steering me towards an ever greater reverence for life. *A Heart on Fire* is my attempt to describe this spirituality, which has taken shape both from my own experiences and from outside influences: people I have met, figures from the past, and books. This is a form of spirituality which sees God as being deeply engaged with the world and not as some kind of superior authority figure observing us from a distance. It is a spirituality in which it is as important to enjoy creation as to protect it.

When I read about the medieval mystics Julian of Norwich, Mechthild of Magdeburg and Hildegard of Bingen, I saw in them this same affirmation of life. It was such a joy to read words written by women who lived hundreds of years ago and to recognise myself in them. It is not always easy to absorb what they say, but just as I have been helped by various authors, so too I hope I can help others to be enriched by the spirituality of these visionaries.[2]

A little about the book:

The first part focuses on how we can meet God within ourselves and what may stand in the way of this encounter. First and foremost I write as a woman who has felt the need to explore images of God that are different from the traditional male ones. Only in this way have I been able to seek out God.

The second part is about the various ways we can perceive the presence of God in creation. I believe we have to bridge the gulf between God and the world which has existed for so long in Christian theology. Seeing God as indwelling in creation helps us regain our reverence for earthly things, a reverence I feel is vital if we are going to be able to address global environmental concerns.

The third part of the book deals with how we can draw closer to and get to know God through our involvement in global issues. In the Old Testament book of the prophet Micah I have found three key words to reflect on here: justice, compassion and humility. My aim is to lay the foundation for a spirituality and a practical approach to life which will help us live with a compassion that embraces people, animals and the environment.

I think many of us long for the kind of Christianity that is engaged and creation-positive: many people are open to testing new images of God when the old ones no longer work for us, and want to be God's tools in the work towards a better world. Let us be brave and determined as we develop this spirituality. We need it. The earth needs it.

Introduction

What does it mean to be a Christian in today's world? People give different answers to that question and to a great extent their answers depend on their background and the situation they find themselves in. It is the same for me too, of course. As someone involved in social issues I feel that the kind of spirituality which takes this involvement seriously has been missing in the Church and in Christian literature. I believe we must build a Christian spirituality that is truly turned out towards the world, following the example of Jesus – and we need to do it urgently. I make my contribution from where I stand in this life: as a 37-year-old woman, a member of the Church of Sweden (Lutheran) with a Catholic background, who feels an affinity with movements whose core concepts are nonviolence and radical discipleship.

It is not only among medieval mystics that I have found inspiration. Women and men of today who are looking for new terminology to use when speaking about God and the world are an inspiration to me, too – theologians whose work is influenced by the reality of this 21st century we are living in, who take global injustices, animal abuse, threats to the environment and other world issues seriously. I feel it is time for a radically different orientation. We need to take a fresh look at God's involvement in creation and at our life as believers. Why? Because a large part of Christian spirituality throughout history has been lacking in two major ways. Firstly, it has been completely absorbed with our inner life and as a consequence has led us away from the holistic biblical view that all our relationships matter. And secondly, it has been people-centred to the absurd extent of reducing the rest of creation to a backdrop for the drama being played out between God and humans.

Many mystics express the view that creation and God are intimately interconnected, that creation flows out of God and exists in God. Mechthild of Magdeburg, who lived in the German town of Magdeburg during the thirteenth century, wrote: 'The day of my spiritual awakening was the day when I saw, and understood that I saw, all things in God and God in all things.'[3] Hildegard of Bingen, an abbess living in a convent in the Rhine Valley during the twelfth century, expressed it in a slightly different way: 'And when people look at creation with sympathy, with trust, then they will see the Lord. It is God which humankind is then able to recognise in every living thing.'[4]

These quotes highlight two different perspectives. When we, as Mechthild suggests, are open to what the spirit of God wants to communicate, we see creation in a new light. And when, as Hildegard says, we relate to creation with sympathy, we are provided with the same insight: the presence of God dwelling in all living things. The two mystics reveal different ways of obtaining knowledge about God and experiencing the closeness of God. One way takes place more in stillness, the other more in action, in relationships. I believe these are two paths which we can walk simultaneously and which offer mutual strength. Traditionally, the emphasis has been on stillness and prayer and that is why I want to promote 'to be in relationship' in various ways as a path to God: going through the different phases of life together with others, enjoying creation with all our senses, meeting others with compassion, and being engaged with life in its various forms. It is all these paths to a whole – holy – life in the world that *A Heart on Fire* wants to explore.

Knowledge beyond textbooks

Scotland, January 2007. The asphalt in front of the gates of the nuclear weapons base glittered with rainwater. It was cold and damp and I was soaked through to my underclothes after a day on the blockade. I crouched down, waiting for the police. All around me they were taking people away. A little way in front of me supporters were standing around a brazier, warming their hands. Behind them, illuminated by the security lights of the base, I could see the high fence with its coils of barbed wire at the top. The fence. Suddenly for me it became a symbol of all violence and everything that sustains that violence. Threatening, yet not invincible. Weapons and violence – there is nothing of God in any of it. It cannot endure.

I felt happy to be there. Obviously it's not pleasant to think about such things as weapons of mass destruction, but it is liberating to come out of that limbo of simply sighing over the state of the world into doing something concrete, not letting discouragement have the last word. I was where I should be. It was good.

How do we get to know God? How do we draw close to God? As I said earlier, prayer and meditation in stillness have frequently been upheld as the principal methods. However, many Christians have also been aware that virtues such as humility, selflessness and love for others need to be practised to become established, and that a life lived in that spirit brings us closer to God. The exercises you will find throughout the book can be seen as a continuation of this tradition. They are about action and allowing ourselves to be influenced by that action. They are outward-looking. They are about our relationships – with other beings and with creation.[5] I believe that practical exercises such as these are a long-neglected way of opening the heart, of opening ourselves to the Holy Spirit.

In the book of 1 John in the New Testament we read:

'Dear friends, let us love one another, for love comes from God. Everyone who loves has been born of God and knows God.' By acting in a loving way towards others we will gain knowledge – not the knowledge found in textbooks but an intimate knowledge, an experience of who God is. This is what I would like to call a theory of knowledge for the spiritual life, and it forms the basis of this book. I feel I have experienced something of this truth in my own life. It was only when I became involved in work for nuclear disarmament that I began to understand the chasm between the God of life and those monsters of death. Only since getting to know women addicts in prison have I been able to be part of God's love for them. Only after coming into contact with animals such as pigs, for example, have I felt tenderness for them, a tenderness which I believe is a part of the all-encompassing divine love for creation.

Many of the exercises in this book will influence our feelings in certain directions – towards wonder, enthusiasm and gratitude, for example. Feelings are very important in our life. Among other things, they have an enormous effect on our thoughts and actions. Think, for example, how hard it is to greet someone with a smile when you are in a bad mood. If we can influence our feelings in a positive direction, so that they support our attempts to live an involved and compassionate life, that can only be for the good.

Rediscovering mysticism

One of the purposes of this book is to demystify mysticism. Mysticism does not necessarily involve spending several hours a day in contemplation, having visions or experiencing total oneness with God. Mysticism is also those moments of wonder, joy and love of life – as well as pain caused by the suffering of others – which we all experience. To be receptive to life and to offer ourselves in the struggle for life is an approach we all can adopt, each in our own way.

The word mysticism comes from the Greek *mystikos* which originally meant 'connected with the mysteries'. In Greek and Roman society it was associated with secret practices in cults, in which only the initiated could take part. Gradually it came to mean 'shutting off one's senses' to search for wisdom in the inner self. It was not until the 6th or 7th century that the word took on a Christian meaning, when a Syrian monk wrote a work called *Mystical Theology*. The phenomenon that the monk wrote about – to still the mind and search for God in your inner self – was nothing new for Christians, however. It had earlier been called contemplation.

One dictionary defines mysticism as 'deep subjective religiosity', but do you have to shut off the senses, and therefore the outer world, to experience deep spirituality? The traditional western view has been that outside influences are a distraction. Asceticism, an attempt to discipline the body and mind, has mainly been concerned with trying to avoid these influences. One example of this approach can be found in a book on spiritual life from the beginning of the 1900s, which describes admiringly how Saint Laurent Justinian abstained from gazing at the beautiful countryside and the trees in his garden, even though he had the opportunity to do so.[6]

That sounds ridiculous to us today. Naturally it pleases God when we enjoy the beauties of creation. Sight, hearing, touch, taste and smell – our senses and all the experiences which come through them are gifts from God. So, do we never need to switch off our sensory perception? Sometimes – and certainly more now than in the Middle Ages – there are too many sensory impressions than are good for us. There is not enough time to work through everything we experience, nor do we have time to listen to our own inner voice, and of course that's not good. But to say that we occasionally need to slacken the pace is a completely different thing from saying that in themselves sensory impressions are detrimental to spiritual life.

I have searched for definitions of mysticism which include this positive view of creation and the senses. One author writes that mysticism is about 'entering the fullness of the mystery of our existence, the gift and blessing of creation itself'[7], and doing this with an openness to the Divine Mystery, the One who sustains all that exists. I think that is a definition of mysticism that opens up in us a desire to live life to the full. My own definition, or working hypothesis, is this: to affirm the divine presence in all creation, including myself, and to act accordingly.

But definitions don't say it all. Another way to approach the issue is to look at the life mystics lead. Most of the mystics and saints we remember today lived their lives as an expression of prophetic involvement: criticising injustice, serving the poor and reaching out to people seen as unworthy. Their life was a part of God's own life, goodness and love which encompasses us all. Theirs are the footsteps we follow, those of us who want to be mystics in the world. The path is not always easy or straight, but there is much joy to be had. It is my hope that more people will discover this path – a path to bring about change in us and in the world.

God within us

Julian of Norwich and images of God

Julian of Norwich is today considered a great theologian. She was an anchoress, or recluse, at the church of St Julian in Norwich, Norfolk. Being a recluse meant choosing a contemplative life in the heart of the city. A person ceremonially entered a cell attached to the church, after which the door was walled up, and that is where the recluse stayed for the rest of his or her life. Their life was not only about prayer in solitude, however. There were windows facing in two directions, allowing contact with the world. One looked into the church, so that she could take part in services and the other looked to the city. People would knock on the window to talk to her and ask for spiritual direction. She usually had one or two servant girls, too; in one text we read about Julian and her maid Alice.

Julian was not actually her real name. It was traditional for those who chose the life of a recluse to be named after the church where they had their cell, so not even the name of this woman is known, or her background, or whether or not she had lived in a convent previously. However, her book remains and it tells us she was born in 1342 and that the crucial moment in her life, the day she received the revelations, took place in 1373, halfway through her thirty-first year.

Julian's text was given the name *Revelations of Divine Love* and it is truly love that holds the centre place as she relates what God showed her in a series of sixteen visions. What also comes across strongly is an assurance that everything lies in God's hands and that 'all shall be well and all shall be well and all manner of thing shall be well'.

Writing in expressive language, Julian describes how much God loves humankind. 'At the same time our Lord showed to me a ghostly sight of his homely loving. I saw that he is to us everything that is good and comfortable for us. He is our clothing, that for love wraps round us, enfolding us and embracing us all around for tender love, so that he may never leave us.'[8]

It is as if she does her utmost to show her fellow Christians how loved they are. I think of how often God's love is mentioned in church services. It's rather a well-worn theme, isn't it? Every other sermon seems to contain the words 'God loves you'. Strangely enough, it often has no effect on me, as if they are merely words. Despite this I still believe that we humans need to discover God's love, so that we can live in it and feel secure in it. The knack is probably to make that love a reality, and in this Julian of Norwich has come to my help. She tells how she came close to God and was overwhelmed by the tender love that radiated towards her. With Julian's help, I want to reflect on the issue of images of God, because I believe the picture we have of God decides to a great extent how we relate to spirituality in the first place.

There was a period in my life when I was afraid of God. For a few years I had experienced a calling to be a sister in a monastic order, but then I felt I had not received enough confirmation that this was the direction I should take. My spiritual mentor recommended that I shelve these plans for a few years and live a 'normal' everyday life. The months that followed were tough. Suddenly the future seemed black and empty. What was the purpose of my life? Most of all, how could God treat me this way? I had been seeking God's will for many years and still he chose not to give me an answer! I was, quite simply, angry with God. I took myself away from my church. I felt ashamed when I was with the sisters, the very people whose way of life I had wanted to follow. And as for praying – well, that was completely impossible. But I remember one occasion when I tried, despite it all. I remember it well because that was the time I saw a picture before me. It only lasted for a second or two, but it was perfectly clear. I saw an axe falling from the sky, directly down towards my head. The rage I felt inside towards God had changed into what I felt was God's rage towards me.

One day, many years later, while sitting and reading Julian of Norwich, there was a sentence that leapt off the page: 'I saw no manner of wrath in God, neither for a short time nor a long,' she writes.[9] This puzzled her. According to the teachings of the Catholic Church, which she followed closely, God showed sinners his wrath and sent them to hell if they did not repent. She reflected on this contradiction for a long period of her life. When she took up her pen again, twenty years after the visions, it was mainly about this she wrote. She had been given a picture from God to help her understand. It was about a master and his servant.

'The lord sits solemnly in rest and in peace, the servant standing by, before his lord reverently, ready to do his will.' The master looks on the servant with love. In a low voice the master sends the servant away 'to a certain place to do his will'. The servant rushes off, eager to carry out his master's wish, but he doesn't look where he is going and falls headlong into a deep ditch, injuring himself badly. Moaning, he tries to climb out, but cannot get a foothold. 'And of all this the great-est mischief that I saw in him was failing of comfort; for he could not turn his face to look on his loving lord, who was very near to him, in whom is all comfort.' He cannot see his master's gaze; he cannot see that it contains only love and compassion. In his deep distress his mind is affected and he becomes confused.

Obviously, the figure of the master is an image of God. The servant symbolises mainly the human being, but also Christ, who is indivisible from the human being.[10] How does Julian interpret the parable? In this context it is interesting to remind ourselves of the kind of society Julian lived in. She was seven years old when the Black Death first came to Norwich and wiped out about forty per cent of the town's population.

After that it struck the town repeatedly during her lifetime. Even if we know nothing of how Julian herself was affected by the ravages of the Plague, she must certainly have personally experienced tragedies in its wake. Political and ecclesiastical structures could not stand in the face of these catastrophes. Violent power struggles broke out. The harvests failed for many years and there was widespread famine. When you consider these circumstances, it is an amazingly positive view of humanity that Julian expresses. The servant falls because he is eager and careless, 'for his good will and his great desire only were cause of his falling'. The image of God is positive too. The pain we feel when we fall is not anything God desires. 'I saw that only pains blame and punish, and our courteous lord comforts and sorrows; he is always to the soul in glad countenance, loving and longing to bring us to bliss.'

'Wrath and friendship are in their being opposites,' writes Julian. And God is friends with us. This was her message of joy.

Another aspect of God's love is goodness. God desires everything that is good for us. Rationally, this is obvious, but even so it can be hard to take in. 'If it is your calling, then you will be at your happiest as a nun,' the sisters often said when I talked to them about choosing my path. I did so much want to believe that, but somehow could not. Did God want to make me happy? Was that really a part of God's plan? Was I allowed to have a good life as well as doing good for others?

Out of fear of where this would take me, I found it hard to hand my life over to God.

According to Julian, God wants to satisfy our needs, even the insignificant ones. 'For he does not despise what he has made, nor does he disdain to serve us in the simplest office that belongs to our body in kind.' 'For as the body is clad in the cloth, and the flesh in skin, and the bones in flesh, and the heart in the body's trunk, so are we, soul and body, clad in the goodness of God.'[11] It warms my heart to read these words from someone I trust as a spiritual guide, because there are others who have also had visions, but who relate different images of God. When I lived in Stockholm I often went to the Roman Catholic cathedral which was close to my student lodgings. Once when I was there I heard a talk about how the Virgin Mary had appeared to people in various places in the world, including to a group of young people in Medjugorge, Bosnia-Herzegovina. (According to their website, medjugorje.org, she appears there still.) To them she said that it was only the prayers of the good people that protected humanity from the wrath of God, as if the prayers held back the arm of God that wanted to strike the earth. After reading this I never again looked at the book I had bought about the apparitions. I felt instinctively that it did not further my life's journey.

In many ways Julian expresses how God's attitude towards us is marked by tender and ardent love. God suffers with us when we fall, when we do things that are less than good, when we take the consequences of our sin, not because these actions wound God, but out of compassion for our situation, as when a parent watches its child act self-destructively. Perhaps it was as a result of this image of God that Julian developed a theology of the motherhood of God. Many before her had written about God as Mother, but no one as comprehensively or systematically as Julian.

Who is God for me as a woman?

I had been a contented Catholic for many years when I first encountered feminism. It was really nothing I myself had been seeking. It came to me by way of new friends. I found myself with my back to the wall when faced with questions about what the Catholic Church really felt about the exercise of power and about men and women. It was painful. At first I tried to find satisfactory answers in the Catechism and other Catholic literature. I asked a friend of mine, a Catholic priest, about it. I tried to work out what I thought myself – for example why women could not be priests in my Church. But the arguments sounded hollow. I discovered that they no longer convinced me. Even so, it was hard for me to step outside the teachings of the Church. After all, I had been instructed in the official teaching, that the Holy Spirit led the hierarchy of the Catholic Church in a certain way when it reflected on questions of faith.

It was only when I came across 'the disobedient Catholics' that I received the push I needed to relinquish my chosen subordination to the authority of the Vatican. I read Werner Jeanrond's *Call and Response: The Challenge of Christian Life* and realised that a Catholic theologian could have an understanding completely different from the official view of how authority within the church ought to function. I read Lavinia Byrne's book about women and the priesthood and was astounded that a woman in a religious order had publicly questioned why women could not become priests.

By this time my eyes had been opened to the tragic history of the Catholic Church as far as its view of women was concerned, and I did further research in order to gain more understanding. When I finally became convinced that the official teaching and the Pope could be mistaken, it was the start of a kind of grieving process for me. I had felt very secure as part of the great community of the Catholic Church, and even if I had no plans to leave the Church I had now given up the comfortable and slightly self-righteous position of 'contented Catholic'. I could no longer accept something just because it was decreed from above, from the hierarchy. I wanted to stand on my own two feet and think for myself, together with all the other Catholics who felt that not everything was right with the Church. There were, after all, quite a number of us who saw serious problems in the way the Church's hierarchy dealt with questions of gender and power.

A depressing example from this time is the Pope's decree in 1994 forbidding any debate within the Church on the issue of women priests.

As well as grief, a huge amount of anger welled up inside me – anger about the history I had discovered and the fact that the Catholic Church of today was not willing to deal with this moral debt. Instead, it did quite the reverse: it tried to sweep it under the carpet. In countless ways the men of the Church have supported and encouraged the oppression of women. Prominent theologians have labelled women incomplete men and doubted whether they actually have souls. That 'the woman' played a greater part in the Fall than 'the man', and therefore women should be subordinate to men, has been preached far and wide. Women's voices have been silenced in the Church; until the 20th century women were not even allowed to be members of a church choir. And on and on. Knowing this background history, the more subtle oppression of current times took on another form for me. It was no longer about the odd theological error. The legacy of openly belittling women – which naturally has no mileage in our modern world – was now taking the form of persistent prejudice and discrimination.

How we see each other as people and what we believe about God are not two separate issues. The question of male and female is central to the matter. In a world controlled by men – and to a very large degree that is still the case – it would be odd if the highest authority, God, were not also masculine. All the Christians I have spoken to confess to the theology of 'God has no gender, is neither man nor woman', but almost all of them still want to talk about God using male terminology. An image of God is deep-rooted. It cannot be changed by pure willpower; it is a process that takes time. I would like to share my experience of that darkness, that spiritual night, which this change entailed in me when it became impossible to continue using my image of God while at the same time lacking a new concept with which to replace it.

The dark night of the feminine

I had realised that man and woman were not equal before God – well, in theory they were, but not in practice. One instance that confirmed this for me was a discussion in my church fellowship about whether girls could assist during services. Traditionally only male choristers have carried out the duties, but around the world Catholic congregations had begun to allow girls to serve. That is the way it was in my neighbouring parish, but in my own church there were those who opposed this modern notion, and the priests supported them. That is not unusual in itself: many people are conservative and never want anything to change. It was their reasoning that upset me – that girls would disturb the boys' concentration by their very presence, or that a more suitable duty for girls would be to decorate the altar before mass.

I thought of the girls who had expressed a wish to become altar servers. How did it affect their view of religion and God to be denied this because of their gender? Why could they not take part in the service in the same way as the boys? Were they not allowed to get too close to God? This entire discussion made me wonder what it was doing to *my* view of faith and God to see only male priests year in and year out. Despite the various arguments put forward in support of this situation, it sends out signals which I believe many women and men pick up on. Only men can represent Christ and hence God, since we believe that Christ is God. God is named using only male images and pronouns. This forges a strong connection between God and men. According to the first chapter of the Bible both men and women were created in God's likeness, but how are we women to interpret this when no female images of God exist in our churches? In what way are we then a likeness of God? Is there nothing female in God?

I often felt despondent when I came out of church after Sunday mass. I began to wonder why I went there at all. Shouldn't mass be sustaining and uplifting for the participants? Gradually I realised that the combination of male priests (and deacons and servers) and a thoroughly male image of God had become unbearable for me. It spoke to me every Sunday and said: 'You are not as like God as men are. God is much more man than woman. Your role in the Church is limited simply because you are woman. But you should be content with your lot!'

It was about this time that I began to consider looking for another denomination with a different view of men and women. I also searched for Christian literature which investigated images of God other than the usual ones. I began to try using female images of God in my spiritual life. It wasn't easy. I recall two different emotional reactions. The first was that certain characteristics of God suddenly became much clearer, especially intimacy and tenderness. The second (and most prominent) reaction was a feeling of being lost and insecure. Was I praying to the same God? Was this really OK? Or was I making 'The Lord our God' angry? They were strong feelings and they stayed with me. It took years rather than months to get over them, to achieve a new feeling of security together with God.

American theologian Beverly J Lanzetta has described the process that many women go through to find a spirituality which affirms their whole person. She calls it 'the dark night of the feminine', adapted from the phrase 'the dark night of the soul', found in a treatise written by the medieval monk Saint John of the Cross (more on this later). Her description of this night stems from her own life and the knowledge she has gained as a spiritual mentor for women. When I read about the experiences of these women I suddenly understood what I had been going through some years earlier.

I had distanced myself from a theology and a spirituality which damaged me as a woman, one that did not affirm the image of God in me. The result was a kind of darkness: I stood in a spiritual wilderness without words or images for the spirituality that I knew ought to exist out there somewhere. A spirituality which would make me whole, which would help me get in touch with God in my inner self, and live together with God. But how was I to find the way forward?

For me it was important to read about women who had gone through a similar process and had come out on the other side, and to talk with friends who were also asking themselves how they should live as informed women within the Christian tradition. It was obvious that everyone had to find their own way. I read of women who had chosen to leave Christianity because they experienced faith and church as hopelessly male-dominated, but there were many others who upheld their place within the Christian church and who retained the more equal position that appears to have been practised during the first hundred years of the church.

In a period of searching such as this it can be simpler to use the language of mysticism, rather than that of theology. Often it is not as prescribed but somewhat more poetic. Mystics are aware that God can never be described using our words. God is beyond terminology, always something else, greater, more different than we can imagine. When Meister Eckhart (1260–1327), theologian and mystic, said, 'I pray God to rid me of God,' I think he was referring to the fact that our perceptions of God often stand in the way of God.[12] Supported by this tradition we need not feel fear as we explore whether our images of God have become a hindrance for us.

According to Lanzetta it is normal to need time to grieve about the oppression and all the resulting suffering that has affected women throughout history and today. Her advice to women going through this process is to spend time in stillness and solitude, and to invite God's spirit in for guidance. Spiritual violence towards women – for example, when girls hear in Sunday school that their sex was responsible for the Fall – can impact on us at a very deep level and it is often hard to describe in words the feelings this triggers. However, to achieve wholeness it is important to bring such experiences up to the surface, to become conscious of how we have been affected and to grieve over the destructiveness involved.

Many have felt that the worst demon in this scenario is a sense of unworthiness. Church and society are full of opinions about how a woman should be, and among them are many attitudes which limit and damage us. In 'the dark night of the feminine' we try to empty ourselves of these images. Then, in the emptiness, God fills us with the insight of our worth and beauty, and we are restored by God's tender-hearted love. Having gone through the night, we feel empowered to become who we really are, and from that stance we can function powerfully in the world.

The fact that I write only about the woman's dark night doesn't mean that men are not also affected spiritually by the way a certain type of maleness dominates religion and society. Perhaps men who find it hard to see God as father and feel uncomfortable with the message of popular culture – that men must be hard, independent and more interested in the outside than what happens on the inside – go through a similar process. Perhaps a man will feel called to write about this. I'll leave it up to you.

Christ as our mother

Julian's images of God are filled with compassion and are not in any way punitive; nor are those of some other female mystics, among them Teresa of Avila, a Carmelite nun who lived in 16th-century Spain. Perhaps they understood that this was what women needed to hear, as opposed to being patronised by society. The traditional view of sin – that it is caused by pride and self-will – has been developed by men and has suited men better (although not all of them, naturally). Women have more often been held back by a lack of self-esteem and have been unable to take themselves and their calling seriously. This is where another theology of sin is called for. Here, Julian's words from the 14th century sound surprisingly contemporary. She does not mention pride or lust or pleasure when she talks about sin. Instead she writes about shame, fear and anxiety. The great problem, according to Julian, is that people so easily become stuck in self-accusation and do not see that God's love is as great for them when they do the wrong thing as when they do what is right. 'If we fall, hastily he raises us by his lovely embracing and gracious touching,' she writes about Jesus.[13]

Julian sees much motherliness in God, and in Christ especially. 'To motherhood as properties belong natural love, gentleness, wisdom, knowledge and goodness,' she wrote. This is what Christ stood for to such an extent that it is actually only him we should call mother, Julian exclaimed. 'The mother's service is nearest, readiest, and surest, because it is the truest,' and only Christ can fulfil this completely. He is always near us to support and nourish us. 'The mother may give her child suck of her milk, but our precious mother Jesus may feed us with himself; and does so very courteously and tenderly with the blessed sacrament that is precious food of true life.'[14]

I think it is liberating to discover how Julian develops this theology about Jesus Christ as our Mother. She was inspired by the Bible and early church fathers, but at the same time she was creative and independent. She relied totally on what was revealed to her, even if at times she thought it went against the teachings of her own church, and the Church exerted enormous authority and influence at that time. Many historians have reflected on the fact that in principle there was only one way for a medieval woman to have a public voice: to give voice to her vision from God. She had no authority in herself; she was not even permitted to express her opinions about church teaching. In the short text that Julian wrote when she was thirty she asked readers not to see her as a teacher 'for I am a woman, ignorant, weak and fragile'. In the longer text, however, written when she was fifty, she no longer makes excuses for herself. She expresses herself with certainty, aware of the knowledge she possesses.

Let us be inspired by Julian when we try out female images of God! It is good to know we are not the first and that we do not have to leave Christian fellowship simply because we want to see the femaleness of God, or speak of God using female terminology.

This concerns not only women's spirituality, but also how we see ourselves in relation to the world around us. We need a God who is intimate and engaged in creation to give us the strength to draw close and be engaged. The traditional kingly image of God is a problem here. I believe the world needs a motherly God. Everyday care and basic needs are still associated more with women than men, more with mothers than fathers. Such care and such spirituality need to be bolstered in a world where millions are even yet starving and living in substandard conditions.

Naturally, the point of having a changed image of God is not to reinforce the stereotypical perceptions of what is feminine and masculine. In a hundred years' time, when men play an equal role in the care of children and the elderly, it won't matter quite so much how we view God in this respect. But it matters now.

So, how did my spiritual journey continue? I can't explain how it happened, but one day I felt secure with God again. The passage of time and listening to other people's experiences helped me to reshape my picture of God. I felt happy and convinced that I was made in the image of God, the way everybody is, and I knew that the God I believed in is one who does not judge and whose prominent characteristics are tenderness and a passion for justice.

I still see God through the lens of the Trinity. I experience God the creator as the foundation of our existence, our origin and our parent, intimate and full of loving care. Often God's face is motherly to me, but sometimes it is fatherly. Jesus has become more important to me, in two ways. Firstly, as the Master and prophet of nonviolence whom I want to follow, and secondly as the Cosmic Christ, the God who lives in the world, present in every created thing (read more about the Cosmic Christ in the chapter titled *God in Creation*). The Spirit is for me a female, life-giving force which helps us to see and comprehend, which guides us through everyday life and supports every good deed.

The other evening I had proof again of how deeply I am affected by feminine images of the divine. I was attending a performance of *Kroppens och innerlighetens mässa (Mass of the*

Body and Intimacy) written by Ingmar Johansson. On my song sheet I saw a couple of lines that astonished me.

'*We have discovered the godperson, she who gave her life for us. Who delivers us from death, that joyful hope. She who rises up from the graves, completely united, one with God. She who dies for us the moment we are resurrected in your light.*'

When the choir sang that verse, I wept. It was a feeling of relief and liberation.

When the mass was finished I questioned Ingmar Johansson about those lines. 'Why not use feminine pronouns for Christ?' he answered rhetorically. 'In Christ there is no longer man or woman.'

We are God's dwelling

At the beginning of the 13th century a women's movement which has fascinated many historians sprang up in Central Europe. At a time when women's liberty was greatly restricted, young women began to form communities and live according to their Christian calling without asking men for permission. They survived on charity and their own work, often some kind of handicraft. They prayed together and they cared for the poor and the sick of the town. Why did they not go into a convent instead? Because at that time it was only women from noble backgrounds who had access to convents, and also a large dowry was expected from anyone joining the convent. Many convents were over-full since they acted as a kind of depository for young women who, for whatever reason, could not marry.

The Beguines, as the women in the new movement came to be called, lived a life that today we would identify as a monastic one, but they took no vows. While they lived in the communities they remained unmarried, but there was nothing preventing them leaving later to get married. From the very beginning the men of the church were frightened by these independent women. How could they be controlled? Even if their way of life was initially blessed by the Pope, many bishops wanted the women either to get married or to join a convent, bringing them under the authority of either a man or the church. Beguine communities were formed in many towns, some of them with several hundred members. Sources of inspiration for the Beguines included the Dominicans and the Franciscans, new orders which also settled in towns and whose friars tried to live a Christ-like life. For a hundred years the Beguine movement blossomed. Many of its members are remembered today, thanks to their writings on spiritual life, but the hierarchy of the church finally put a stop to the movement by claiming that the Beguines' spirituality was heretical. In 1312 a ban was imposed: all the communities were to be closed or integrated into a monastic order.

In 1230 a 22-year-old woman arrived in the German town of Magdeburg. Her name was Mechthild, and she had left her home and come to the town to live as a follower of Jesus. It is likely that she soon joined the Beguine community that existed in Magdeburg, and there she stayed for many years. When she was in her forties she told her spiritual mentor how she had been experiencing the divine presence of God ever since she was twelve years old. He encouraged her to write down her experiences, which she did, and the little we know about her life is contained in the introduction of that book. The book was lost for years but was rediscovered in a convent library in 1861.

Much of what Mechthild has written is difficult for a modern person to comprehend. She writes about her relationship with God in words of courtly love (characterised by a man beseeching an unattainable woman), common in the spiritual literature of the time. Despite this, many aspects of her spirituality speak to me. She describes God's love as continuously flowing towards us. *The Flowing Light of the Godhead* is the title of her book, and 'flowing' is probably the word that occurs most frequently in her text. Using different images she describes the overflowing love we live in. We are floating on God's breath, she writes, as birds glide in the air on still wings. In one vision she saw four streams of light radiating unceasingly from the triune God. 'There is no one, rich or poor, who the rays do not touch in love. They are shot through by the unfathomable light of the Godhead.'[15]

I like the fact that there is a mutuality in the love relationship she describes between God and humanity. God is just as thirsty for love as Mechthild. 'I cannot live without you,' God says to the soul. 'You are my gentle pillow, my most beloved bed.' God has enough of everything. Caressing souls is the only thing God cannot get enough of.

So what is a person's soul? Do we even believe we have a soul? Previously it was thought that there was a space within every person where the soul fitted. Now we know there are no cavities in the body; it is filled with organs. We have thoughts, memories, desires. We know those exist in the brain, or have their origin in the brain. So is that the seat of the soul? Today, researchers think that the self is perceived through the dimension of time, 'when the frontal lobes organise our life on the axle of time, minute by minute'.[16]

Most people, however, would put their hand to their heart if asked to describe the soul, and in Christianity the heart has traditionally been considered the centre of a human being. We love with our heart, we suffer with our heart. But we can also say that the soul exists in every part of the body. That point of view agrees with today's holistic perspective of the human being. We are *besouled* bodies, not soul *and* body. That is, the soul is the nucleus of my person. It is merged with the body and expresses itself through the body.

However, the mystics maintain that *within* the soul there exists a special place. It is there that we become one with God and, through God, one with everything and everyone. Teresa of Avila describes this centre as a sun. 'We notice here that the source and this radiating sun which is in the centre of the soul never loses its lustre and beauty. This *always* exists deep inside the soul and nothing can deprive it of its beauty.'[17]

Just think, this something within us never loses 'its lustre and beauty'! Whatever we do, whatever happens to us. Theologian Beverly Lanzetta asserts that this is the central understanding of the mystic view of humanity, that 'the core of our being is untouched by sin and belongs to God'.[18] She highlights how empowering this insight can be for many people, for example women who have been victims of sexual violence.

We who have not – yet – experienced this core have to trust that it exists, that it is a reality. Since it is a spark of the reality that is God, through it we can also understand something of God's being. This is made clear in Mechthild's book: she uses the same images for both God and the soul, those of a soaring eagle, fire, sparks, sun, rays of love.[19]

When Mechthild was awoken by love, she saw and understood that 'God is all in everything', but she was mainly preoccupied with God's presence in the human being, this presence that she felt so clearly. Julian, too, was filled with joy that God lived within her. 'And then our Lord opened my ghostly eye and showed me my soul in the midst of my heart.' It was as large as a kingdom and built like a city. 'In the midst of that city sits our Lord Jesus,' and he 'shall never, without end, leave the place that he takes in our soul; for in us is his homeliest home and his endless dwelling.'[20]

God is in the soul but the soul is also in God. Mechthild describes this in her characteristically lyrical way: 'The mind of God and of the loving soul come together in the same manner as the sun and the air unite through the majestic energy of God in a sweet vibrant mixture in which the sun overcomes the coldness and darkness of the air, so that one notices only that it is all one sun.'[21]

Mechthild found herself in an exposed position. She was a woman who maintained that the Holy Spirit inspired her words, a Beguine who publicly criticised corrupt priests and bishops. We understand from her book that she received a great deal of criticism and perhaps even abuse. 'Those who appear to be good people stone me from the back and run away.'[22] In her sixties, tired and ill, she found refuge in the Helfta convent, a more secure place than the streets of the town. The Benedictine nuns who lived there showed a great deal of interest in mysticism, and they welcomed her. There she stayed until her death.

God in me? It is hard to understand. Often we feel so alone. How can that be if God exists within us? There is a simile for

God within us: God is like a spring of clear water, but if the water is rarely used then with time twigs and leaves will collect on its surface and hide it. Can that be right? I believe it is the same as with everything in a person's life. The things we do seldom or never are difficult, while the things we do often become easier with time. Nerve impulses create a path. If I decide to believe in the inner spring where God exists, then I give God the opportunity of meeting me there.

Exercise
Face the fear

Face the fear that might arise when you try to relinquish a non-functioning, hurtful image of God, but do not allow it to hinder you.

- Try using different names for God. Muslims say that God has 99 names. Perhaps they are better than we Christians when it comes to naming God creatively. As I have said, it can be hard to discard names and along with the names the images that we have grown up with or heard so many times in church. Feel free to find ways of describing God that are relevant to your experience and give you joy and comfort. Love, Mother, Sister, Foundation, Living Water, Holy Wind, Friend, Lover, Passion for Justice, Creative Energy ...

• Share your thoughts with others. Discuss the process with them, read books (see suggestions at the end of this book).

Exercise
The inner sanctuary

If it helps, think of the place where you and God unite as your inner sanctuary. Use it. In periods of silence and stillness we find a quietness which we can then bring to mind during the activities of the day. This is also a way of confirming our belief in our own worth, and in God. I am like 'a beautiful sun' in God's eyes and God wants to 'caress my soul', as Mechthild expresses it. God wants to be together with me.

Silence is onerous for most of us. We are not used to it. Even if we can appreciate outer silence, we find it hard to still our thoughts. Our heads are full of chatter. We fear the silence inside, wondering what might come up. Personally, I have felt a vague fear of discovering an emptiness inside me. What if there is no one there? But then I think of Julian's words, 'in us is his homeliest home'. God is at home in me.

Another reason modern people find meditation and prayer difficult is that we live inside our heads so much, but stillness and company with God is not something we should think our way to. How can we shift the focus from the head to the heart? We do that through the body, according to Anthony de Mello (1931–1987), a Jesuit priest who lived in India. Remember, we are besouled bodies. In and through the body we can still ourselves, open ourselves up to the divine presence and just be together with God. Two ways of doing this that de Mello recommends are through our breathing and by being aware of sensations in the body.

- Put aside 10-15 minutes every morning and/or evening. Begin by moving your body a little. Bend forwards to the ground and then stretch up to the sky. If you have the opportunity and a little more time, yoga is a good preparation for stillness and prayer. It can also be a prayer in itself.[23]

  Sit comfortably, on a prayer stool or chair. Sit in an upright position, as if someone were pulling on a string from the top of your head towards the ceiling. If you want to, hold your hands together or close your eyes.

  Do the following breathing exercise: Breathe in and say quietly to yourself, 'In one.' Breathe out and say silently

'Out one.' Breathe in, 'In two.' Breathe out, 'Out two.' Continue to ten and then count back down to one. This is a good way to come into stillness. If you start to think of something and lose count, start from the beginning again. Continue to be in your breathing, noticing how it feels. Do not control it. Feel your stomach moving in and out. If you like, think 'in' and 'out' with each breath. If you find you are distracted by many different thoughts, take three really deep breaths and then just be aware of your breathing again, without influencing it.[24]

After 5-10 minutes, simply be still and put yourself and the day/night into God's hands.

● Alternatively, do the following exercise to transfer your concentration to the body.

Sit comfortably. Close your eyes. Notice how your clothes rest on your shoulders. What does it feel like? Can you feel your clothes against your back? Can you feel your thighs pressing against the chair? Now to your hands: how does it feel when they are resting against each other, or against your legs? Now your feet. Can you feel them resting on the floor? Be in each sensation for a few seconds, then move on. Repeat this circuit several times. Then choose a small area of the body to focus on, your forehead or chin, for example. See if you can feel any sensations in this area. If not, go back to being aware of the various parts of the body, as above. Then return to your chosen area of the body and try again. Repeat this until you do feel something in that area. What does it feel like? Itchy, prickly, stinging, throbbing? Stay in that feeling for a while.[25]

Finish by being still and open to the presence of God within you.

• God lives within you, but embraces you also. You live in God, you move in God. So incomprehensibly large is God's heart that all beings find room inside it.

Imagine you live in God's heart. Visualise God's love with the help of Julian's image: it wraps you round and encompasses you, just as clothes enclose the body.

Continual intimacy. Motherly tenderness.

'It is high understanding to see and to know that God who is our maker dwells in our soul; and it is a higher understanding inwardly to see and know that our soul, that is made, dwells in God's substance.'

Julian of Norwich[26]

God in creation

Some years ago a friend told me that she had been to a Christian meeting and had got into conversation with a fellow Christian from another denomination. When she told him about her involvement with Amnesty International, he said: 'But what does your church say about that?' My friend, who is active in the Church of Sweden, was very surprised by the question. When I asked her what she thought he meant, she answered: 'I suppose he thought that I ought to put all my efforts into doing church work.'

I was extremely upset by this attitude. Later I wondered why I had reacted so strongly. Amnesty works for people who are in very vulnerable situations: unjustly imprisoned, often tortured. How can anybody, Christian or otherwise, not think it important work? How can someone who is a Christian not see it as work inspired by God? I think what lies behind this outlook is the old division of worldly versus spiritual. My friend ought to focus on her own church because it is Christian congregations that carry out 'God's work' – that is how I interpreted the man's question.

I believe it is often this attitude, which polarises the 'material' and the 'spiritual', that is to blame when people experience church services as irrelevant to the world. This only really became clear for me when I came into contact

with the Iona Community, a widespread Christian fellowship
with a centre on the island of Iona, off the west coast of Scotland. When I reflected on why their services and prayers felt
so right and relevant, I discovered it was because prayer, social
issues, biblical figures, people's everyday lives, environmental
concerns – all were included in a united oneness. It seems
obvious, but there are historical reasons why this holistic
approach does not come naturally to us Christians.

For the past three hundred years we have lived with a
mechanistic world view. We are so used to it that we don't
even realise that it *is* a world view. The difference between it
and the earlier, organic, view of the world, which lies nearer
the mystics' experience, is huge. In that view, we all fit
together, with nature, with each other. Nature is alive and
humans are aware of their dependence on the earth. The rapid
development of science during the 17th century struck the
death blow to this approach to life. Scientists believed themselves to be distanced from the world and they studied it as if
it were a dead object. For them, the world was one big
machine: if something wasn't working it could be repaired. In
this outlook God risked becoming the ultimate fixer, not
involved in the life of creation on an everyday basis but only
intervening to resolve crises.[27]

There has been a division between body and soul, between
earth and heaven, from the early days of Christianity, influenced by Greek philosophy. There was a hierarchical order in

the universe and anything concerning the spirit or the soul lay eternally above the material as something purer and more meaningful. This view is known as neoplatonism, inspired by the ancient philosopher Plato.

At the time the letters of the New Testament were written, around the year 100 AD, the whole universe was still included in meditations on God's salvation. It was not just about the human soul; no, everything that existed in heaven *and* on earth was encompassed by Christ, according to these writers. In Colossians I it says: 'For by him all things were created; things in heaven and on earth, visible and invisible, whether thrones or powers or rulers or authorities; all things were created by him and for him. He is before all things, and in him all things hold together.'[28]

Soon, however, the focus moved from the cosmos to the Christian Church, God's dwelling place on earth, and from there to the individual Christian. Augustine (354-430) has heavily influenced Western Christian spirituality. He was not interested in cosmic perspectives, but rather those of psychology and the sin and redemption of the individual. This type of theology didn't make the same impression on the Eastern Church. There it is emphasised that the whole of creation is involved in God's actions. With the knowledge we have today about the universe, this point of view appears much more relevant and productive.

A living universe

'There is more to wonder at than we could ever dream of,' writes Ulf Danielsson, professor of theoretical physics, about our universe. Much of what has taken place in science, not least within physics, during the past decades leads to wonderment. Time and space are connected. Time has various speeds depending on place. There are not only four dimensions – three in space plus time, those we live in everyday – but perhaps eleven.

If we are striving for the right approach to the world around us then we need to listen to these discoveries. Our curiosity about the Creator demands it. We need not be afraid of what is going to be revealed; as Jesus said, the truth will set us free. The old dichotomy of science versus religion feels distant when so much beauty, logic and elegance is being discovered by those who explore the world and, interestingly, the dialogue between scientists and theologians has intensified during the past 15-20 years.

One cause for surprise is how perfectly matched are biological conditions and the laws of physics to allow for the creation and sustenance of life. To take only two examples: if any one of the mathematical equations regulating the universe, such as how great the gravitational force is in the nucleus of an atom, had been a fraction different, planet Earth would not have existed.[29] And if the share of the

atmosphere's oxygen were to rise above the 21% it constitutes, all vegetation would be destroyed because fires would
not burn themselves out.[30] The composition of the atmosphere depends on the interplay between living beings, plants
and micro-organisms. Plants produce the oxygen we need
and we produce the carbon dioxide the plants need. That this
complex system works is fantastic.

It is easy to find parallels between a mystic understanding
of the world and the modern, scientific one. One example is
the extent to which all the parts of creation are interconnected and dependent on each other. And this is true not only
of biology. Physicists have carried out a particular experiment
several times and reached the same amazing result on every
occasion. Two electrons which have been separated and sent
off in different directions still have some kind of communication with each other. When one of them is evaluated the
other one is immediately affected, despite the huge distance
between them. One interpretation physicists have made based
on this knowledge is that reality on a fundamental level is an
indivisible unit. Physical and biological processes cannot be
explained by looking at the sum of the processes of the individual parts. Rather, it is that the totality in some way exists
within each part, like a kind of consciousness.[31]

Physicists cannot provide us with proof that God exists; it
is not possible to observe God in that way. However, for those
of us who are believers, the researchers' discoveries become a

pathway to seeing new aspects of God, and the creation which reveals God to us.

An incarnate God

Icy winds were blowing around Scan's abattoir in Linköping on that February morning. I was there with five other Christians concerned about animal welfare, to pray for animals in the livestock industry. We had placed an icon of Christ and some pictures of suffering animals and people against the wall with a couple of candles in front of them. We sat silently on camping mats. From time to time an animal transporter passed a few metres behind us. Suddenly it became completely obvious to me: of course God feels the animals' suffering deep within God's own being! Of course every individual matters to God. How can we humans fail to understand that?

The following day I read in the newspaper that a cow had escaped from Linköping's slaughterhouse earlier that morning. She had just been unloaded from the truck when she jumped over the fence and ran off. For one and a half hours she ran through the industrial area and local housing estates. After a while she had four police vehicles chasing her. On the way down to Lake Roxen she was caught. And killed.

In the chapter *God within us* we looked at the importance of images of God. Now I'd like to return to that subject, but from a different perspective: God's relationship to creation.

Christianity's relationship with the physical body is divided. On the one hand, it is a religion in which God – or a part of God – becomes one with humanity by being born as a human being. On the other hand, 'God the Father' has been portrayed within traditional Christianity as disembodied, as pure spirit. That God is spirit perhaps sounds obvious to us. Who believes that God has a body? But as we shall see there are other ways to approach this question.

I have already mentioned the influence of neoplatonism and how it contributed to the elevation of spiritual matters and the abasement of earthly ones. The traditional emphasis on life after death, eternal life, has reinforced this emphasis on the spiritual. How can our bodies and earthly things be important? After all, we only live on this earth for a short while.

I – and many with me – have felt that this is not right. Life here and now *is* important. What we do with our own and other peoples' bodies *is* important. It is certainly important to God. The fact that the Iona Community's songs and form of spirituality have spread across Europe can perhaps be seen as a sign that more and more people share this feeling. In many churches in Sweden renewal work is going on. New song texts and prayers are being written. More importance is given to world affairs and everyday life, and that is very good, but we also need to take a step back and ask ourselves how we actually see the relationship between God and creation. Can it be that the fundamental viewpoint of the theology we rely on actually counteracts our efforts? I believe it does.

Traditional Christian theology states that God cannot be changed. Plato asserted three hundred years before Christ that the highest good must be perfect and therefore changeless, and the church fathers adopted this way of thinking. God loves creation, certainly, but not in a way that God risks being affected fundamentally. Nothing that happens on earth perturbs the peaceful being that is God. What kind of relationship is that? Can anyone be intimately connected with someone else without being affected by what happens to them? No, for us as human beings that's impossible. And, according to more and more theologians today, it is also impossible for God.

In traditional Christian belief God exists outside creation. Of course, earth is a place where we can meet God in many ways, but creation and God are two completely different entities. The earth can be destroyed but God would remain without any problem. In this way of thinking, God lives primarily in God's own domain, heaven.

Naturally such a theology does not inspire a burning interest in the earth and its inhabitants. If God is independent of creation and is not actually affected by it, then why should we Christians devote our energy to changing the world?

I was happy when I discovered the trends within current theology which distance it from these ideas; women and men – for

example Marcus Borg, Carol P. Christ and Jay McDaniel –
who dare to steer their thinking about God along new tracks.
Their sources include biblical tradition, their own experiences
and new scientific discoveries about creation. They assert that
God is totally oriented towards relationship, that God is in an
intimate relationship with each and every created being.
These relationships affect God deeply. God suffers with those
who suffer, rejoices with those who are happy, and despairs
each time an individual is subjected to violence. In one way
God is perfect and changeless, they say. God feels perfect sympathy. God is continuously undergoing those feelings and
experiences that every being goes through because God is
present with us, in us. Bringing this world into being was a
huge risk for God, considering the freedom each individual
has to choose not to live a life of goodness. God's very being
is affected by all the destructiveness on earth.

The image many of these theologians use to describe the
relationship between God and creation is 'the world as the
body of God'. The image tells us that what takes place in the
world takes place in God. These experiences – of peoples, animals or cells – are as intimate to God as my body is to me. It
means that God is the soul, the consciousness, the very heart
in the body that is the universe.

But can there then be any freedom for us humans? My arm
does what I want it to do; it can't act independently. This is
where the picture slips a little, despite the fact that the cells in

our bodies don't always do what we want them to (for example, when we are ill or injured).[32] It seems to me that this direction within theology – the one influenced by process philosophy – takes free choice more seriously than many others. We really are co-creators with God. God rejoices at our creativity and freedom in the same way as a parent is glad to see a child develop and take responsibility for its life. The consequence of this attitude is that the future becomes uncertain – for God, too! Since God knows everything and everyone, it is God who has the greatest possibility of divining the future. But not even God can see it in detail, because the development of life on earth is dependent on how we human beings choose to act.

I believe this point of view frightens many people because the logical conclusion is a God who is vulnerable. A God incarnate. It involves a major rethink of our ideas to abandon the independent and almighty God, the one who could choose to intervene and change everything in the blink of an eye, if so inclined. God does not have that kind of power. I would rather have the God of love than the God of power. The one who is involved, who feels. The one whose heart is on fire for creation, in creation.

A God who reigns in the heart of everything

'God is in all things, yes he reigns in the very heart of all things,' wrote the medieval theologian Thomas Aquinas.[33]

The mystics also experienced that God lived in creation. As I wrote earlier, the image of the world as God's body is one way of explaining this reality. God inhabits creation just as we inhabit our bodies. This statement is not entirely uncontroversial among Christians today. Many have a fear of finding themselves embracing Pantheism, which places a metaphorical equals sign between God and creation. However, the point of view that I am trying to put across is called Pan*en*theism: the belief that God inhabits creation and that we – everything and everyone – live in God. Panentheism is not a new concept. Martin Luther expressed this view when he wrote that 'God is substantially present everywhere, in and through all creatures, in all their parts and places, so that the world is full of God and He fills all, but without His being encompassed and surrounded by it. He is at the same time outside and above all creatures.' [34]

Julian of Norwich saw God not only as being present in all things but also as the driving force in the world. 'See, I am God. See, I am in all things. See, I do all things. See, I never took my hands from my works, nor ever shall, without end,' she heard God say.[35]

To want to emphasise God in the world is not to deny God's greatness. Quite the opposite: it is to allow different aspects of the divine to complement each other. Let me give you a few examples. The Eastern Orthodox tradition talks about God's essence, which is God's transcendence beyond creation, and God's energy, which is God manifest through creation.[36] Meister Eckhart challenges us to 'see God in all things'. At the same time he talks about 'the godhead', by which he means God beyond all things, even beyond the Trinity. Sallie McFague, an American professor of theology, writes that even if 'God's body' is visible to us through creation, God's face is always hidden from us.

To whatever extent God indwells in creation, God is also always beyond it, greater than it.

The presence of Christ in every atom

In 1984 a discovery was made that would change the suppositions of physics. Researchers gained a completely new perception of the smallest particle of everything that exists – something so small that no microscope is capable of revealing it to us. Suddenly gravitation could be integrated with particle physics (the laws which control the most minute particles). Physicians from Einstein onwards had struggled without success to do this. The new approach was to think of these small units as vibrating threads. Depending on how they vibrate they build up different constituents, such as electrons and protons, which in turn combine to form atoms. These threads, or strings as they are called, vibrate in a way that is not at all coincidental, according to physicist Brian Greene. He says that their behaviour helps us better to understand the laws of time and space.[37] These strings are not only components of fixed matter but also of all forces, such as electro-magnetism and gravity.

Even before string theory the matter-energy division had shown itself to be untenable. To our minds a table and magnetism seem completely different things, but there is no basic difference; they consist of the same components. This knowledge is revolutionary. Would Plato, Augustine and others have devalued matter if they had known what we know today? They saw matter as something dead; how could it then have a close relationship with God, the most Living of the living?

Through the discoveries of quantum physics we can have a new perception of the presence of God in creation. Everything consists of vibrating energy. It is these patterns of resonance which decide what the world consists of. With this knowledge, writings from the Middle Ages speak to us in a way that their authors could never have predicted. I am thinking, for example, of Hildegard. 'Without God's WORD no being exists,' she wrote. God's WORD, Christ, is indwelling in everything created. And this is how she described the relationship between God the Creator and Christ: 'All creation is awakened, called, by the resounding melody, God's invocation of the WORD.'[38]

The theology Hildegard follows, that it is Christ who dwells in creation, gives us a slightly different perspective. Her source of inspiration is the teaching of incarnation. This doctrine, one of the most important in Christian tradition, has mainly been interpreted as God becoming human in the form of Jesus of Nazareth. Within the mystic tradition, however, many have offered a more comprehensive view of incarnation. Meister Eckhart stated that God is incarnate in us all.[39] Others, such as Hildegard, have meant that we can talk about God's incarnation in the whole of creation. Pierre Teilhard de Chardin (1881-1955), a Catholic priest, geologist and mystic, agreed: 'Christ, through his incarnation, is internal to the world,' he wrote, 'rooted in the world, even in the very heart of the tiniest atom.'[40]

Without losing the link to the earthly Jesus, Teilhard wanted to expand the Christian's understanding of Christ. He wanted to open peoples' eyes to the universal Christ, the Cosmic Christ, which is Christ incarnated in all bodies, in all material, in the whole cosmos. He wasn't saying he had discovered something new, rather that he had brought together the New Testament theology that everything is created in and through Christ with scientific insights about the universe and the earth. He was concerned that his church was inward-looking and obsessed with rites and structures. Perhaps the time has come, he wrote, to 'rescue Jesus' from the hands of the priests 'so that the world can be saved'.[41]

For Teilhard the world has a heart, and it is Christ who is that heart. He is 'a furnace of fire' at the centre of the universe.[42] The divine fire which burns in this heart, at the centre of every created thing, is an eternal, unending source of spiritual energy. This fire of love is the strongest and most transformative power in the world, wrote Teilhard, and we can be a part of it by identifying ourselves with it and living in love.

'The creative work of God does not simply mould us like soft clay. It is a Fire that animates all it touches, a spirit that gives life. So it is *in living* that we should give ourselves to that creative action, imitate it, and identify with it.'[43]

The Christian image of God is recognised as a belief in God as the Trinity, three persons in one God: the Father/Creator, the Son/Deliverer and the Holy Spirit/Life-Giver. How does that belief fit with the images of God we have considered? Teilhard visualised a picture of the Trinity's inner life, in which all created things existed in the very centre. He was convinced that the entire cosmic process – evolution – strives towards God the Creator through Christ, in the Spirit.[44] This picture is similar to Hildegard's view: God calls upon Christ in creation and in doing so draws all of creation to himself. We are all drawn into this vibrating interplay between the Creator and Christ.

The melody resonates in our cells.

The world as the body of God, and the Cosmic Christ: these are two perspectives to inspire us. For me, they give faith a whole new dimension. Spirit and matter become so much more exciting when they are united. As Teilhard wrote, they are two aspects of one single cosmic tapestry. It was hugely liberating for him to be able to mentally demolish the barrier that his teachers and others had erected between spirit and matter, and to understand that matter in no way stood in opposition to spirit, or was its enemy.[45] What this actually means is, I feel, unclear for most of us. I can sit on my balcony and look at the birds in the trees and ask myself, 'How is God in them?' I can watch a documentary on television about quantum physics and different types of energy and forces and wonder, 'Is this how God works in the world, through these forces?' Despite all the unanswered questions, the earth and the universe now appear more alive to me, and God comes very close when I see Christ as the heart of matter, the heart of creation.

Ruth Dahlén: A Swedish mystic

In 1946 a Swedish woman called Ruth Dahlén had a vision while out skiing in the south-west of Sweden. She has described this and other revelations in her book, *Visionär i tjugonde århundradet* (*Visionary in the Twentieth Century,* not translated). Her experience of the inner nature of reality provides an image that links to both Teilhard's divine fire of love and the vibrating strings of quantum physics.

'My eyes were fixed on an unusually beautiful snowflake

which had landed softly on a pine needle. Suddenly something happened to the pine needle: it dissolved in flickering flames of light, infinitely more intense than the sun's light, but not dazzling. The waves of light appeared to move with dizzying speed in a kind of spiral motion inside the pine needle, which still retained the shape and character of a pine needle.

'Pine needle after pine needle was lit up by the flickering waves of light. Soon the forest was aflame. For a second I was absolutely terrified – had something happened to my brain? Then I distinctly heard a voice speak to me from a distance, not a normal human voice but still a voice, absolutely clear and distinct: "Do not be afraid. Keep your eyes open and observe carefully what you are going to see!" Immediately I became completely calm, very happy and expectant. Soon the entire forest was a sea of the same living light, alive in a way which makes normal earthly life almost lifeless in comparison. I, too, had become a figure of light; I looked at my hands, which were able to grasp the boughs of the burning pine tree, and they were of the same transparent light. The whole of creation vibrated with these incredibly fast rays of light, in which I could clearly distinguish every individual ray, see how it worked ...

'I saw the cosmos functioning in five dimensions, not static but dynamic; there were the three dimensions of space, time was a fourth and there was also a fifth dimension, the constructive, unifying dimension, the inner mystery of the universe,

Love. I also saw this LOVE as streams of light particles, spreading in spirals throughout all creation, a chain reaction of enormous pulse beats, a cosmic breathing process.'[46]

Ruth Dahlén was well read in other religions, especially Hinduism, and wanted to promote a greater understanding between eastern and western thought. The basis of her own experience was 'a cosmic consciousness emanating from a personal being'. She felt she could discern this basis in the words and concepts of many religious traditions.[47] In this calling from God, as she understood the visions to be, she realised she was to work towards unity between all who believed in God and alert the church to the threat of the destruction of the environment. She felt, however, that the church did not take her message seriously.

The future of the earth

What do we think is going to happen to this planet? Some Christians doubt that it will be a part of the future kingdom of peace, at the end of time, but in light of the theology we have discussed that appears to be a strange position to take. Would God really reject this universe which has taken so long to develop? And if the cosmos is God's body it seems even more strange that it would disappear, or be changed into something completely different.

The debate about end times can be interpreted as a continuum with continuity at one end and 'something completely different' at the other. How much will remain roughly the same as it is now? And how much will be totally changed?

According to the Bible there is an alliance between God and all created things. God entered into that alliance with humankind and all the animals at the time of Noah. A reasonable interpretation of this covenant is that God is not going to abandon the earth and its inhabitants. Julian of Norwich understood that creation would endure in some way. She heard God say: 'I will re-establish everything in its right condition. I am able to do this, I intend this and I shall do this.'[48]

Teilhard de Chardin might not even have understood the question. In his work as a geologist he explored the history of the planet, and for him it was obvious that creation would evolve towards an ever-greater complexity and higher consciousness. He was aware of the importance of evolution. Knowledge of evolution has given us a completely new perspective on the history of the planet. We know that life on earth has evolved over millions of years. We know that it is incredibly richer now than when bacteria and algae were the only organisms on the planet. We know that for most of earth's history there was no conscious life here. Naturally our knowledge about this process of growing complexity and consciousness influences our spirituality. That was Teilhard's message. It appeared to him as if all matter is evolving towards a greater unity. The final goal for this development is, according to Teilhard, the Omega Point, or Christ-Omega. This is the point where Christ draws all things into himself.

Teilhard is not alone in seeing the impact of evolution on Christian life. Other theologians, too, have realised that we must take this understanding of the long history of the cosmos into account. One author writes that evolution corresponds well with the biblical view of time.[49] The books of the Bible recount the idea of a promise inbuilt in the world and time. The greatest is yet to come. God will meet us from the future.

But what, then, happens to humanity's role and responsibility? Will this development lead us to Christ however much we destroy our planet? That's a serious question. God draws, entices, creation in a certain direction, but of course we humans have our own free will and in using it we can really put a spoke in the wheel. The planet's destiny lies perhaps in our own hands. Will it be something wonderful? Or just okay? Or something that is God's emergency solution – a plan B?

I believe that we have already destroyed God's plans for the earth. Humanity has exterminated many animal species and ravaged environment after environment. Climate change will only exacerbate this progression. But I also believe God's reforming energy can salvage something good from the situation.

For Julian there was no doubt about the future of the earth. In her first vision she saw the world from the outside, as small as a hazelnut.

'Also in this he showed a little thing, the size of a hazelnut in the palm of my hand; and it was as round as a ball. I looked upon it with the eye of my understanding and thought: "What may this be?" And the general answer came: "It is all that is made." I marvelled as to how it might last, for I thought it might suddenly have fallen to nothingness, because it was so small. And I was answered in my understanding: "It lasts and always shall, because God loves it; and so everything has being by the love of God."'[50]

Exercise
Conscious presence

To be present – that is a prerequisite for the rest of the exercises in this book. We can't be moved by gratitude, see beauty or have a better understanding of the world unless we notice what is around us. We can practise this and become better at it, but we all operate within a different set of circumstances. If you have practical worries, such as how you are going to manage financially, you will probably find it harder to be in the present because of the anxiety occupying your consciousness.[51]

To live consciously means living in the now, and that is not easy. Our thoughts churn around and flit first to the future, then to the past. I have experienced an egotistical tie to my thoughts when I have practised conscious presence. I find I don't want to let go of them. Our thoughts do not always work for our own good, however. They are often trivial: how well I have done certain things, what others think about me, what I want to do in an hour's time, and so on. It can only be beneficial for us to let go of them from time to time.

- Begin by choosing a particular time of day to practise being present, such as when you are getting ready to go out in the morning. Notice how your body feels when you sit up in bed, how you walk to the bathroom, how you breathe. Try to do one thing at a time and do it well, with all your concentration.

- Let certain events or occasions act as an alarm clock for you to be present, to take a few deep breaths and give thanks for the time which is now, this very moment. It could be when you get into the car or onto the bus, when you sit down in front of the computer to start work or at the table before eating.

- Practise looking at things without judging them or having

thoughts about them. Don't think about what use the object can be to you. Simply take it in just as you see it. Everything God has created has a part in God's being. Perhaps you will be able to perceive, if you devote time to an object, how oneness with the Divine shines through.

- Try to discover something new every day, or see something familiar in a new way. If you live together with others, tell each other in the evening what each of you has noticed during the day.

'Every single creature is full of God and is a book about God.'

Meister Eckhart[52]

Exercise
Wonder

Practising wonder is all about combating the emotional bluntness caused by our society of excess. As children we have a natural curiosity about the world. As adults we have to actively support this curiosity so that it doesn't fade away among our other plans and projects. So often we walk around lost in our own thoughts without noticing what is around us. Wonder is about perceiving reality as it is, because beauty exists everywhere.

If we practise this outlook it will strengthen our desire to explore the world further. Use your senses! Smell, feel, taste, look, hear. Make some time for this in your everyday life. And if it causes your pace to slow down a little, that might be a good thing in itself.

- Touch leaves, flowers, and other natural things. Pick them up, examine them.

- Be open to beauty in unexpected places: patterns in the pavement, an old person's face, a fly cleaning its wings.

- Go with a child on a journey of exploration. Allow yourself to be filled with joy at the things you discover together. Don't be afraid of being childlike.

- Read a book about the origins of the universe and the earth.

'If I spent enough time with the tiniest creature –
even a caterpillar – I would never have to prepare a sermon.
So full of God is every creature.'

Meister Eckhart[53]

A tender touch

It was late afternoon when we reached the cottage where we were going to spend the night. It was a cold April and Les from England was amazed that there was still snow on the ground in many places. Our group of about sixteen people had been together for four days and the atmosphere was relaxed. We were celebrating 'Easter in the footsteps of the unarmed Jesus' by walking from Örebro to the Bofors weapons factory in Karlskoga. The following day we were to meet some of the factory's employees and plant vines on the premises – vines as a symbol of security and peace, according to the prophet Micah and other biblical texts.

Although it was only Tuesday in Holy Week, the theme of the day was Jesus washing the feet of the disciples. The question we had reflected on during the day was: What does it mean for us today to be each other's servants? We gathered in small discussion groups. Joel from the US told us how he had experienced a feeling of being able to be 'a Christ' for the other prisoners during the times he himself had been in prison.

It began to get late. A couple of chairs were brought to the front and a bowl of water and a towel put beside each one. We sat in a large circle singing Taizé songs. Those who wanted to could go forward and sit beside a bowl or on one of the chairs, to wash someone's feet or have their own washed. For a long time, no one went forward. Then someone plucked up the courage and others followed. It felt unusual to touch someone else's feet, but it was beautiful. I felt tenderness. When my feet were washed I was both moved and grateful.

To show care for someone else's body – isn't that a test of spirituality?

Exercise
Reverence

Reverence is about seeing and affirming the divine presence in everything and everyone. It's about allowing this approach to have repercussions in your daily life. Touch earth, trees, plants; they are a part of God's beautiful body. Appreciate fresh water and the air which gives you life. Think about how you treat your body. Think about how you treat other people's bodies.

Sometimes it's hard for us to summon up feelings of reverence. In that case let your actions – your hands – express reverence for you.

- When you meet someone you find difficult, remember it is the same God who lives in you both.

- Meditative cooking. Try to make sure you are not disturbed while preparing food. Think about how you handle the raw ingredients and do so respectfully. Thank God for each ingredient, for the soil it grew in and the people who sowed and harvested it. Enjoy the aromas and experience the different textures.

- Collect creation-positive verses or prayers to read in the countryside. Write a sentence or two on a scrap of paper (a quote from Hildegard or Meister Eckhart, for example, or from someone else in this book). Carry it with you in your bag and take it out and read it from time to time when you are outdoors, as a way of reminding yourself of the holiness of creation.

'Who is the Trinity? You are music. You are life. You are alive in everything and yet you are unknown to us.'[54]

Hildegard of Bingen

The power of love

Passion has not exactly been a suitable subject of study in the history of the Christian Church. This has to do with the view about emotions in general. Leading theologians have been influenced by Greek thought, which placed reason above all else. Feelings were dangerous and could affect your reasoning. Love was divided into different kinds, among which Eros, connected to passion between two people, was often portrayed as egoistic, while Agape, the highest form of love, was unselfish and pure.

The picture is not straightforward, however. There were also authors, among them Origenes (ca 185-254), who spoke of humans being in love with God and having a passionate love for God. When you have travelled far on the spiritual path, he wrote, and purified your longing by asceticism, you could have a 'love sore'. This sore burns with the 'blessed fire of God's love'.[55]

Another inheritance from Greek philosophy, one which still exists today, is a negative connection between women and emotionality. One of the many weaknesses of women, in the view of men in the church, was their very connectedness to their emotions. According to German theologian Dorothee Sölle (1929-2003), it is this view of emotionality that has contributed to emotions being excluded from theological reflection to such an extent. (And today, when many theologians are women, we see a much more frequent interest in how our emotional life and our spiritual life influence each other.)

Female mystics *have* involved their feelings; they have used them in the service of love. According to Elizabeth Dreyer, professor of religious studies in the US, this is something the medieval women mystics can teach us. They are passionate in their longing to serve God and people. They allow their passion to drive their love and involvement, without necessarily giving less importance to knowledge and reason. 'Love without knowledge is as darkness for the wise soul,' wrote Mechthild.

One of these passionate mystics is Hadewijch of Brabant, a Belgian woman who lived in the 13th century. Many of her writings have been preserved, but just like Mechthild she was forgotten for several hundred years. At that time girls from wealthy families could receive an education, either at home or in a convent school. Hadewijch was one of these educated girls and she later became a superior in a Beguine community. She had a passionate relationship with *Minne,* which meant Love in her Dutch dialect. She uses this word with a capital letter to indicate God, but *minne*, with a lower case *m*, is also for her 'the divine power which permeates existence'.[56]

Her love relationship with God involved a great deal of pain and despair. The longing for closeness to Love was very strong, but often Love was absent, or subjected Hadewijch to certain trials. 'It matters not how much Love has disappointed me, I must follow her even so, for she has completely devoured my soul, from the depths of my heart. I shall follow her completely and utterly.' But joy with the relationship and the hope of being one day united with Love was always with her. She placed her life in Love's hands. 'I trusted completely in Love, since the first time I heard her named, and I handed over myself to her power.' Service to her fellow human beings remained important to her and she warns those who think they have come a long way along the spiritual path against losing their eagerness to do good deeds. She challenged her fellow sisters – and us – to give ourselves over to this love relationship, despite the revolutionary effect Love can have on our life. 'Oh soul, creature and noble image, risk the adventure! Consider your law and your nature – which must always love – and love the best good of Love.'[57]

Exercise
Passion

- Don't be afraid to express, to yourself and others, your enthusiasm about something. The word *enthusiasm* comes from the Greek 'en theos', which means 'in God' and can be translated as 'God within us'. In certain Christian contexts enthusiasm has not been a positive concept and it was feared that enthusiastic people were influenced by spirits other than God's. I believe the opposite is true and that we need many more Christians who affirm enthusiasm. Ask God for enthusiasm in your work in the world.

- Value keenness! Thank God for your zeal. Dare to see passion for justice and peace as a part of God's nature. A theologian has suggested 'Passion for justice' as a name for God. Contemplate that.

'I will give you a new heart and put a new spirit in you; I will remove from you your heart of stone and give you a heart of flesh.'

Ezekiel 36:26

Hildegard's vision

'Beginning in the 10th century, increasing during the 11th century and flowing like a powerful river between the 12th and the 15th centuries, we find texts written by women,' writes Rosemary Radford Ruether in her book about medieval mystics.[58] There is very little remaining from earlier centuries. Ruether interprets this as a consequence of women being forbidden to teach publicly. The writings of educated and holy women were not preserved because they were seen as private notes. So what was it that changed during the Middle Ages? According to Ruether it was all to do with the development of convent life. In the convents women were taught to write in their mother tongue and in Latin. There they had access to libraries and writing materials, and daily prayers, using Bible texts, provided them with a comprehensive education in the Scriptures. Often their writings were only meant for their own communities but they were copied by the nuns and passed on to others.

Hildegard of Bingen lived almost her entire life in a convent. She was the tenth child in a wealthy family. At this time Christians were expected to donate to the Church a tenth of everything they were given and earned and this was the reason Hildegard was handed over to a convent when she was eight years old. As a child, she had already begun having visions, in which she saw detailed images and heard them interpreted into

Latin, but it was not until she was forty years old that she told anyone about her visions and was encouraged to write them down. She was at that time the newly appointed abbess of the convent and continued in that role for the rest of her life.

There are many differences between Hildegard and both Julian and Mechthild. Hildegard was declared a prophet and mystic during her lifetime, for example. Prominent churchmen gave her their support and that allowed her the freedom to go out and work in the world. She travelled around, speaking in public in a way few women in the history of the church have found possible.

Hildegard's writings deal with creation and the Fall, patriarchs and prophets, Jesus becoming man, Christian duty in her own time, the End Time and much more. Naturally, it is impossible to sum up her theology in a few lines, but something that attracts the attention of people today is her positive view of creation. She describes the whole cosmos as being filled with God's creative force, a life-giving 'greening' power: *veriditas*. All created things work together in harmony, because God has 'arranged all things in the world in consideration of everything else'.[59] There is a mutual love between Creator and created which she compares with love and faithfulness between husband and wife. All the beauty God pours into creation Hildegard sees as a divine kiss.

Exercise
Connectedness

A central theme in the mystics' writings is that 'oneness' between God and everything created is the most real reality. Perhaps that's not so strange. Mysticism is often described as a journey of the soul where the destination is unity with God. But then creation, too – the good in creation – is included in the experience of unity. This oneness does not mean that our individual character is an illusion. We exist as individuals and each and every one of us is distinctive in our own way. Ruth Dahlén experienced this in her vision of creation. 'In this world of myriad rays my being was a clearly defined ray, a colour all its own in a continuously changing spectrum.'[60] However, as individuals we have an intimate connectedness with God and, because of that, with every living thing. According to Hildegard it is the Holy Spirit that takes the form of this reality. 'You are the mighty way in which every thing that is in the heavens, on the earth and under the earth is penetrated with connectedness, is penetrated with relatedness.'[61]

Most of us do not experience the world in this way. For us, each person appears as a defined unit; we see ourselves as clearly separate from each other and from the world. I believe that is why we sometimes find it difficult to understand the mystics' experience. It might help if we thought of oneness as the underlying reality. It is not visible to us every day but we know it exists. As we have seen, learning more about modern physics can also help here.

Everything rests in God. The presence of Christ binds us together.

- Look into the eyes of an animal. Try to imagine what it is like to be that animal.

- Look into the eyes of those you pass on the street. Smile. Think good thoughts for them.

- When you buy something, think of those who have taken part in its production. Those who have sown and harvested, packaged and transported.

'Just as a circle embraces all that is within it, so does the Godhead embrace all. No one has the power to divide this circle.'[62]

Hildegard of Bingen

God in engagement

When I was 16 I travelled to Paraguay as an exchange student. For one year I lived with the Rotela family in the capital city, Asunción. The father of the family owned a metal workshop, the mother was a dentist. They had a good middle-class life. After a couple of months I joined a youth group in the local church. We met once a week, read the Bible, discussed things together and became involved in various social projects. This is where I met Any, who remained a close friend for many years afterwards. Whenever I returned to Paraguay I stayed with her. She lived with her mother and her grandmother in a little house near the church and here the standard of living was something else entirely: one room where everyone slept, a toilet at the back of the house, only cold water.

During my first year in Paraguay I thought a lot about the different living conditions of people around the world. Although I never saw extreme poverty it was obvious that not everyone had what they needed to live a decent life. There was an older woman who lived alone in a shabby, dark room next to our house. If the mother of the Rotela family hadn't taken dinner to her every day she probably would have starved to death. Many people had no medical insurance and fared badly when they became ill. I planned to train as something useful – a midwife, I thought – and come back to work with and for poor people.

That didn't quite happen. I did go back after I had trained to be a nurse, and worked for a few months in a hospital, but I didn't end up being a charity worker. Even though I went on to more advanced nurse's training, I wasn't very happy in nursing and left that career a few years later. Nonetheless, I have carried my experiences from Paraguay with me: the feeling of urgency – if there are people who don't have what they need then we must do something about it – and a longing to devote my life to meaningful activity. I hope I am less naïve today than I was then. Then I didn't see the political connotations, nor what it was that prevented people from rising up out of poverty. I had the attitude that as long as we worked together, issues would be resolved.

Meeting people who live in different circumstances is good for us and helps us develop a perspective on life, but we don't have to travel to South America to do that. One way is to get to know people in our own countries whose experience of life is different from ours: people who have fled oppression in their home country or who have grown up in poverty and who perhaps still have family members whose lives are affected by this distress. Everyday life is a battle for survival for very many people. I think that when you live in a rich country awareness of these problems can easily become theoretical. It needs to be brought to life by meeting the people concerned.

We have to question a mysticism that does not lead to increased compassion and an involvement in issues of justice – that has been the message from many spiritual people throughout history. There is something self-evident about this. If God is the love that flows through every creature and the whole of creation, and we are receptive to this God, then our heart will be opened more and more to the suffering of others, and we will be affected by all situations in which humans or animals are not treated with love.

Priests, ministers and authors of inspirational literature often insist that prayer affects our actions in this world. Seldom or never do we read that work for justice is a way into God's heart, and that's a pity, because I believe it would be a liberation for many Christians who feel themselves drawn primarily to this way of knowing and serving God. I also believe it is a part of our biblical inheritance. When the prophet Jeremiah warned King Jehoiakim about God's judgement if he continued to oppress the poor, he reminded him how Jehoiakim's father Josiah had had a completely different way of ruling. '"He defended the cause of the poor and the needy, and so all went well. Is that not what it means to know me?" declares the Lord.'[63]

Spiritual growth is complex, but I am convinced that our actions have a deep effect on our inner life. Luckily there are theologians today who offer a broader approach to gaining an understanding of God, and how we are connected to God.

The British Catholic Anne Primavesi, for example, wants 'to establish physical experience and practical works as both a source and an expression of God-knowledge.'[64] Through action, our own and that of others, we can learn to know God better.

God is like a parent, tenderly loving creation and longing for justice for all God's children. Our calling is to enter into the same attitude towards the world and ourselves. When we act with reverence for the rest of creation and when we struggle so that all may live a life of dignity, we come closer to that which is holy. We come closer to God.

Ethics of mysticism

When Martin de Porres (1579-1639) saw injured stray dogs on the streets of Lima he took them back to his monastery cell to care for them. The other monks protested, calling them 'filthy dogs'. When George Fox, founder of the Quakers in the 17th century, received a divine revelation and became convinced that there is 'something of God' in every person, he became an advocate of pacifism. Although he and many Quakers after him have been punished for their refusal to take part in war, they have stood fast by their belief that they should not cause harm to anyone.

Before we take a closer look at how justice, compassion and humility can be guidelines for spiritual life in the world, I would like to reflect on the characteristics of that engagement with society which is an expression of mysticism. What should be its hallmarks? What is the ethical outcome of a mystical approach? To simplify the question I would like to summarise the mystics' message in three points and consider the ethical consequences of each.

God lives in everything and everyone. What will be the consequences for my life if I choose to trust this mystical wisdom? I think it should be the same for us as it was for George Fox: that it changes our entire way of life and puts us on a collision course with many of the world's norms. It means that reverence becomes the blueprint for how we relate to the world around us. We know to value earthly things because, in Hildegard's words, 'there is nothing created that does not contain a ray of [God's] radiance, not foliage or seed or flower or any other beautiful creation.'[65]

Just as Fox saw something of God in every person, we can see something of God in every being, thanks to the increased knowledge we have today about animals' emotions and their capacity to feel pain. We see how animals take delight in the pleasures of life and we acknowledge that their joy of living, just like ours, comes from God. We see their physical beauty as an expression of God's creativity. Like the Peruvian saint Martin de Porres we see animals as God's children, and as such our brothers and sisters, and go to great lengths not to harm or kill them, striving instead to be their protectors.

One consequence of seeing God in everything is that we are drawn away from the fateful division of reality into worldly and spiritual. Our lives, with all their life-affirming constituent parts, become holy. Or rather, we discover the holiness which has always been present. Gardening, social work, cooking, care of bodies – reverence leads us into a right attitude towards each other and towards creation.

All living things belong together and are connected. How are we to interpret this view of belonging? Do I have a greater responsibility for someone because I feel we belong together? If so, why? I don't think this works as a moral principle. Even if we are completely separated from each other there should still be solidarity between us. However I think we will be encouraged enormously if we dare to believe in the connectedness of everything. It helps us to identify with others, especially those with whom we don't feel a natural affinity.

We can also find support today in the way physics interprets the world. In a purely concrete way all the parts of creation are connected. Every particle belongs to one single global wave function because they have all at some time during history worked together. Therefore each particle's destiny is inseparably connected with the whole of the universe.[66]

God's relationship to the world is stamped by intimate love. Knowing this gives us courage in our work towards a better world. Everything is encompassed by love. That means we should never give up hope for a person or a situation. 'See, I lead everything to the end to which I ordained it from without beginning by the same might, wisdom and love by which I made it,' said God to Julian.[67] Often we don't understand how a situation can be resolved, how good is going to triumph, but our task is to persevere, trusting that God's love will finally bring everything to its completion.

Faith in God's eternal and constant love also forbids us to condemn other people. Nobody is a hopeless case. We cannot support policies that say certain people do not have the right to live or ever be released from prison. We have taken on board the mystics' view of humanity: one part of us is always worthy, always beautiful before God, whatever dreadful things we do.

Remember joy

The Ploughshares Movement is an international peace movement which campaigns for disarmament using nonviolent civil disobedience. When I joined this movement I discovered a new way of working. Their approach was a mixture of the alternative meeting methods of the women's movement and the spiritual decision-making processes of nuns and priests. Several Catholic priests and nuns took part in the first

Ploughshares groups. They brought with them a form in which reflection on a text (often a biblical text) and silence were important ingredients. The women's and peace movements contributed with tools to promote participation, such as go-rounds, in which the delegates speak in turn and no one is interrupted. The result was a calm process where each individual had plenty of time to work out his or her feelings and thoughts. Even though the activities that were planned and carried out could lead to a certain amount of stress – for example, disarmament actions potentially resulting in fines or imprisonment – I experienced the process in our group as both fortifying and surprisingly easy. It involved every part of me – my worries, desires, spirituality and political considerations.

I was probably a little spoilt beginning my political engagement in this way because when I later participated in other movements which had more traditional methods of operation I often found it frustrating. Main meetings were always very time-consuming and even then not everyone had an opportunity to express their opinion. There was the difficulty of getting to know people when small groups weren't used, or were short-lived. Engagement and private life were kept separate and we were not encouraged to be personal. I felt stressed and found the work joyless. I think that the different working methods are partly to do with spirituality. In the Ploughshares Movement a spirituality remains, even though many activists today would not define themselves as religious or spiritual.

In many ways I have experienced what you might call a mystical attitude within the peace movement. Joy and celebration, silence and worship, symbols and rites – all this has had an important place.

At a peace camp in Washington DC during the summer of 2000 there were about forty of us who travelled to the Pentagon, the headquarters of the US Department of Defense. We wanted to draw attention to their responsibility for the sanctions which were so badly affecting civilians in Iraq. A couple of women had prepared a rather unusual litany. While we sat on the wide steps which led up to the entrance, and as the police vehicles began to arrive, they slowly read words from a long list of all those items which could not be sent to Iraq because of the sanctions: cleaning materials, pencils, heart lung machines, pharmaceuticals, and so on. The assembled people joined in with a repeated refrain.

We have walked for days on pilgrimages, often with a weapons factory as our goal. A pilgrimage is a time for both conversation and quiet reflection, at the same time as being a political manifestation. Sometimes Buddhist monks and nuns from the Nipponzan Myohoji order have accompanied us. Their prayers and the regular beat of their drums encouraged our steps when our bodies felt heavy. At our second trial in England, following a disarmament action against British nuclear weapons, one of the nuns turned up outside the court every day. She prayed in front of a picture of Hiroshima in ruins after the atom bomb.

On the mornings of the trial we walked in a procession through the town, from the church which was our gathering place, to the court. In the square outside the building we formed a large circle and sang a song, and someone would explain what was going to happen during the trial that day. To finish we would remember people killed or imprisoned because of their work for justice and peace. We were told their name and a little bit about them, then we all answered together: '*Presente!*' ('present' in Spanish).

At every Ploughshares trial a party is organised and at our trials in England there were several. People take the opportunity to meet up; often they come from many different countries to show their support. The spirit of community and the resistance to violence is worth celebrating.

The activities and systems we oppose have an overwhelmingly destructive power. It is easy to lose courage. But there is another danger, that of being affected during the struggle by the very things we are fighting against. The danger of losing our compassion and creativity. Of starting to divide the world into good and bad. Of letting the end justify the means. That's why we need to arm ourselves with all the good tools available to us, including mysticism. As you can see from the examples above, I don't feel this has to be specifically Christian. It can be Buddhist, Jewish, a general spirituality, or from another tradition. The most important thing is that we help each other bring out the power and joy that exists in spirituality: the hope of a better world, belief in the power of love, the knowledge that we all belong together as sisters and brothers.

So, search for methods and activities which you find give you strength – and say no to those ways and means which drain you of your power. Enjoy life even in the midst of your campaigning! If we can't have fun while we work, we won't last long in the struggle for good. Moreover, life is not just about work, however meaningful it is. We need to relax at times, too, by doing something completely different. For me that can mean coffee and a pastry in a café, or a shot of humour from a TV series – *Friends* is my favourite – to end the day.

'What is good'

Haschem wanted to show us the garden first. The vines had been hacked away but branches remained clinging to the veranda roof, although most of them had dried out. One day the settlers who owned the house above his had come down, their automatic weapons slung over their shoulders, and started sawing through the vines. They wanted to frighten the family and make them move away. Haschem didn't dare stop them. He pointed to a piece of tarmac: that was once the driveway to his house. There had been a time when it was possible to get a vehicle to the house. Now the settlers had taken over the road and Haschem's family had to use a winding track instead.

The city of Hebron lies on the West Bank, 35 kilometres south of Jerusalem. It is a holy place for Jews, Christians and Muslims: the graves of Abraham and Sarah can be found here. I worked in Hebron as an accompanier for a few months in 2004. The Ecumenical Accompaniment Programme is part of the work of the World Council of Churches. People are sent to Israel and Palestine to help prevent violence by their presence and to offer support to those who work for a just peace. Our remit in Hebron consisted of accompanying Palestinian schoolgirls to and from school because youngsters from the Jewish settlement on the same street often threw stones at them. The settlers in Hebron are known for their fanaticism and violence and there is dislike for them also among Israelis.

In this town 2700 years ago you might have come across Micah, a man who criticised the oppression by those in power of the poverty-stricken residents. 'Her rich men are violent … They covet fields and seize them, and houses, and take them.'[68] He is remembered today among Jews and Christians alike as a great prophet.

In Micah's book in the Bible we also read his words about the peaceable kingdom. There will come a time when everyone will 'walk the Lord's paths'. Then people will beat their swords into ploughshares and no longer train for war. Everyone will sit secure under their own vines and fig trees, and no one will terrorise them any more (Chapter 4). The trees will give protection from the wind and the heat of the sun and provide the people with figs, grapes and wine, symbols for all the necessities humanity requires. The earth will be tilled with ploughs, bent swords now serving life instead of death.

There is a passage in Micah which is often quoted in addition to the verses about the peaceable kingdom. It is from chapter 6, verse 8. In the introduction to the book of Micah in one Swedish Bible translation, *Bibel 2000,* you can read that this verse 'somehow summarises the message of the prophets of the Old Testament'. In that case this is an important text for those of us today who try to embrace a prophetic approach to life and society. I would like to look at these words in more detail and offer a personal interpretation of what they have to say to us.

In the preceding verses, the prophet asks about the right way to approach God. Is it through sacrificing calves and rams in their thousands? Is it by 'endless rivers of oil'? (Oil was used for cleansing and anointing and for lamps.) Or, as the Canaanites were said to do, by sacrificing one's own children? The answer to these questions is a resounding no. For: 'He has showed you, O man, what is good, and what does the Lord require of you?' What is the only thing God requires? Songs of praise or communal prayer? To gather together in the house of the Lord? No. The only thing God requires from us is 'to act justly and to love mercy and to walk humbly with your God'.[69]

Of course there are various translations of the Hebrew text. The first point, *'to act justly'*, is sometimes translated as *'to do justice'*, or, as in the Contemporary English Version, *'see that justice is done'*. I assume it means that we should work for justice.

The second point, *'to love mercy'*, is sometimes translated as *'to love kindness'*. The word translated as mercy/kindness is the Hebrew *hesed*. It has been difficult for Bible translators to find an equivalent term in English. What is often missing in translations is the active quality of *hesed*. It involves coming to the aid of those who suffer. I choose the word compassion here, because I feel it conveys this meaning better.

In the last section of the sentence, '*to walk humbly with your God*' is often used in English translations. As I believe that humility is a central theme for those of us living today, I have chosen to focus on that.[70]

Perhaps these attributes can be the foundation stones for a life lived in the spirit of the prophets: to work for a just world, practise compassion for others and allow the spirit of humility to help us find our place in the world.

And because Jesus was inspired by the prophets, it can also be a way of following him.

> *For justice* – Jesus stood up for the weak and downtrodden on numerous occasions, even if it cost him dearly.
> *For compassion* – Jesus reminded the people what God wanted: mercy, not sacrifices.
> *For humility* – Jesus lived a simple life and spent his time and strength on caring for others.

Working for justice

I came into contact with the peace movement just over ten years ago. At that time I had been a practising Christian for thirteen years but despite that had never come across the 'justice perspective'. I had heard in many sermons about loving your neighbour, giving to those in need, etc., but never had this wisdom been put onto a political plane. Faith should have nothing to do with politics, some say. I'm sure that's right in certain circumstances, but because politics concerns the governance of our common life it is hard to keep the Christian viewpoint outside of it. It is about people's right to a decent life, our stewardship of animals and nature, the needs of the weak and much more. It was the same in Paraguay: the congregation kept the moral teaching on a personal level. Together with the youth group I visited orphanages and leper colonies. It was a faith that had social rather than political implications. It was only when I met Christians in the peace and solidarity movements that I understood it was a dimension that had been lacking. And what does this dimension involve? Well, I think it involves seeing the wider meaning; daring to look at how our lives interconnect, south and north, men and women, poor and rich. Observing how we affect each other, and the delegation of power in our relationships. Poverty, for example, is not a natural state. It is mainly created and upheld by political decisions on a local, national and global level. The interests of the different parties in the world are in conflict, and rich nations have institutions to protect their own interests. These often make decisions that do not benefit the poorest people of the planet.

A lot has happened during the last ten years, thank goodness, and popular movements have put global justice on the agenda. But for many Christians this perspective still seems problematical. I have heard young Christians sigh deeply when describing their attempts to bring up these issues in their own churches. Even simple suggestions such as using fair trade coffee at church can result in protests and anger. Perhaps it's time Bible classes studied the prophets?

Justice comes first on Micah's list. For the people of Israel, to act justly was fundamental to their belief; it was a crucial aspect of being a faithful Jew. The same word for justice as in the Micah quote is used by the prophet Jeremiah when he speaks God's word to the king. There it is obvious that the term refers to how we relate to the weak and those worst off in society. 'Do what is just and right. Rescue from the hands of his oppressor the one who has been robbed. Do no wrong or violence to the alien, the fatherless or the widow and do not shed innocent blood in this place.'[71]

Where do we stand when it comes to violence and oppression? 'Do no violence,' wrote Jeremiah, but also: 'Rescue from the hands of the oppressor the one who has been robbed.' It's not enough that we say no to violence ourselves, even though that can be a good place to start. As an individual I have to consider whether in my everyday life I contribute to violence or oppression, for example through the goods I buy or how I invest my money. But as communities – churches, associations – we must also ask ourselves how we can intervene when we know that others are suffering violence.

The knowledge gained and methods developed in the nonviolence movements around the world can help us. Nonviolence means intervening against violence and oppression without using violence ourselves. Quite the opposite: all parties are treated with the greatest respect.

As a basis for working with justice, which naturally takes many forms, I would like to suggest that we espouse a theology of nonviolence. The values of nonviolence will strengthen the spiritual dimension of our engagement.

We acknowledge all people as sisters and brothers.

We distance ourselves from violence and disrespectful treatment of others, whatever their actions.

We have a friendly attitude towards those who oppose us.

We intervene against destructive behaviour and activities and are prepared to take the risks that are always involved when violence is confronted. We put ourselves at risk rather than let others be harmed. In that way we have the opportunity to break the spiral of violence.

It is this – intervention – that is the active aspect of non-violence. In the chapter about compassion we will return to the subject of nonviolence and its basic premise: not to harm or kill.

When it comes to working for justice, exercises like those in this book are not the most important thing, but rather that we practise in real life, working for a better world in any way we can. See the section at the end of the book if you would like suggestions on how to get involved in working for justice.

And remember, for a mystic the focus is not on the result. If we focus our thoughts on success, or if we demand visible results for our actions, then we have entered the struggle according to the norms of this world and have already lost. The mystic knows that she or he is a small part of a greater whole where God's spirit works together with all people of good will. We can only do our best and leave the rest to God.

The power of anger

Anger as a force for change is under-used in the praxis of community life,' writes the English theologian Mary C Grey.[72] The Christian values of meekness and the ability to withstand suffering are not really compatible with expressing anger, she believes. As I mentioned earlier, expressions of emotion have generally been met with suspicion in many Christian circles.

However, feeling angry is a sound reaction when we see others suffering oppression and violence, or when we are affected personally. Perhaps, when it comes down to it, we need to feel angry to access the inner strength necessary for bringing about change. What is anger, actually? Beverly Harrison, retired professor of Christian social ethics, says that it is a marker: we react when things are not satisfactory in relation to others. It is a sign of resistance within us against something taking place in our social relationships. Getting angry means we care enough to get involved, so it is not a feeling that should simply be repressed. Naturally, this does not mean that we automatically act in a morally correct way every time we get angry; to do that demands ethical reflection and practice, for example. Harrison feels that the fear of anger in our churches has had serious consequences. Repressed anger will make itself felt in other ways, such as depression, low energy levels and self-righteousness. The power of love and the strength to take action wither away.[73]

Exercise
Anger

- Bring up the subject in your church. Are there ways you can help each other to acknowledge the anger that injustices create? Would you be able to do that during the services?

- Notice when you yourself get angry. Our anger is not always righteous indignation over an injustice; it can also be caused by a dented ego. By studying your own anger perhaps you can learn to distinguish between different types of anger. If it is a result of something not being right in your life or in the world, try to use the anger to give yourself the energy to act constructively.

Getting in the way

The seminar had several prominent participants, such as Kouichi Toyoshima, a physics professor from Japan, and Professor Sir Richard Jolly, former Assistant Secretary General of the UN. Also attending were university lecturers from Great Britain, the US and Sweden. There were a number of students, too, including myself. Everyone had turned up on this January day in 2007 to take part in a cross-disciplinary discussion about nuclear weapons. Only the location for the seminar was a little unusual: the entrance to the nuclear weapons base at Faslane in Scotland. On this occasion these researchers not only wanted to give their views on the damage weapons of mass destruction can cause; knowing the dangers of such weapons, they also wanted to disrupt the daily operations of the base, which is home to the UK's nuclear Trident missiles.

After an introduction at the entrance we moved the seminar onto the road itself. The huge gate was closed and from inside the base we heard over the loudspeaker: 'The north gate is temporarily closed.' The statements of the participants continued. The police, who were carefully monitoring the events, seemed to listen to the contributions. Some local supporters went among the participants offering chocolate and biscuits. The damp Scottish air made its presence felt and there were only short breaks in the rain. People sang and students from Oxford University performed a play by Shakespeare.

Then the police began walking around, warning us: 'If you don't move you may be arrested.' Most of us stayed put. Police vans drove up and one by one we were loaded into them. Our van drove to the police station in Clydebank and we were held there, three to a cell. I ended up with Kathy, a lecturer from the University of Edinburgh, and Elena, a philosophy student from Sussex. Over our evening meal, a vegetarian lasagne, we chatted about why we had come to the blockade and conference. Kathy told us she had been active in the early '70s in the anti-Vietnam war movement. Elena thought it was cool to meet someone who had been involved back then.

At ten o'clock the following morning we were allowed to leave.

Sometimes we have a moral duty to act even if we are not directly involved in what is happening. The phrase 'third party' is often used: the one who is not the perpetrator or the victim but who is present and witnesses an injustice. It is when we are the third party that we have the greatest chance of stopping what is happening. It might be when we see someone bullied at work, when a child in the school playground thumps another child, or when a soldier mistreats an old man at a checkpoint and we are there as international 'witnesses'.

Intervention can also be relevant in completely different situations, however, such as the destruction of the environment, arms export, and deportation of asylum seekers who risk torture in their own countries. When other approaches have been tried and it comes to a question of life or death, it may be our duty to use our physical body as a barrier.

Exercise
Intervention

- Practise saying no and stopping oppression in everyday life. Calling something by its proper name can be very effective. For example:
  'I feel violated when you joke about my involvement.'
  'I think it's wrong to talk about her when she's not here.'

- Something to think about: Can you imagine yourself blockading nuclear weapons bases or arms exports? Contact an organisation involved with these issues and find out more.

'The Lord looked and was displeased that there was no justice. He saw that there was no one, he was appalled that there was no one to intervene.'

Isaiah 59:15–16 NIV

The prison of consumerism

The theologian Dorothee Sölle uses strong words when she speaks about consumerism. She calls it a prison whose foundation stones are globalisation and individualisation. These two trends reinforce each other; actors in the global market are not interested in local contexts, the 'social and ecological webs' people live in. It is 'homo economicus', economic man, the system wants – an individual who concentrates on business and pleasure and shows no interest in 'the antipersonnel mines his car manufacturer produces or the water his great grandchildren will drink – not to mention any interest in God'.[74]

I consume, therefore I am. That's how deep it goes. Consumption engages our souls, our imagination. It can be seen as a kind of false mysticism. People are not so much tempted by individual products as by a lifestyle which they can be a part of, the new person they can become. And you will never be finished – it's a lifelong project. Whether you can afford to consume more than your basic necessities or not, you can't avoid the lure of the bait.

I can see three serious problems with consumerism. It affects us spiritually by impoverishing our souls and our creativity; it is built on the oppression of people who are exploited in factories so that we can have cheap goods, and of animals, too; and its unrestrained exploitation of resources destroys the environment.

Our resistance strategy has to include fellowship with others, imagination and lifestyle. We have to promote a reverence for creation as a central value in our communities. We have to value simplicity and develop 'the good life' outside the prison that is consumerism: sharing time together eating, experiencing nature and joining in cultural activities. This alternative is not so attractive if we regard it as asceticism; it is preferable to view it as freedom. We will be set free from the straightjacket of created needs and will have time and energy left over for doing other things. The fact is that every purchase is directly related to the amount of time I have to spend working to earn the money for it. In the long term, less money going on consumption frees up time for relationships or something equally important.

Exercise

Liberate yourself from the prison

- Make up your mind not to buy any new clothes for a period of time. Tell your friends about your decision and the reason behind it.

- Buy fair trade goods with some of the money you have saved by reducing your consumerism. Then you will know that your action has helped people to live a decent life.

- Have you got money invested in stocks and shares? Do you know what kind of activities your money supports and how the profit is made? Try to find out. Choose ethical investments. Or ask concrete, ethical questions at the company's annual meeting.

- 'Love of money is the root of all evil,' it says in 1 Timothy. Take a moment to reflect on your relationship to money and possessions. Could it be that your material assets are holding you back in life, from working for justice, for example, or developing your compassion? Are they taking time which could be spent doing more meaningful things?

- Form a small group (if you are not already in a house group or similar) where together you can look at how consumerism influences you and what you can do about it.

Developing your compassion

A central premise of this book is that we can all live in accordance with mystical wisdom – the knowledge of the oneness of all things and God's presence in everything and everyone – whether we have experienced these truths on a personal level or not. To want to believe, and to act accordingly, is one way to a spiritual life in the world that is open to all of us. One of the most significant outcomes of the mystics' testimonies is nonviolence: not to hurt or kill sentient beings. I say significant for two reasons: nonviolence as a way of life is found in all the great religious traditions, and choosing nonviolence makes concrete demands of us and challenges us in our relationships with flesh and blood individuals.

Both Hinduism and Buddhism emphasise *ahimsa* as a fundamental ethical guideline – that is, behaving in a way that does not harm any living being.

To avoid causing any living creature pain is one of the five main pillars of the Jewish faith.[75]

Christian mystics have perhaps said less about nonviolence but it has been practised. The early Christians put themselves at risk of death rather than join the army and be given the order to kill someone else. Many stories are told about medieval saints who saved an animal from being hunted or dying from cold.

There is a story told by the Muslim mystic Bawa Muhaiyaddeen about a hunter who shot a deer and was about to kill her fawn when it suddenly spoke to him. 'God has created people and animals from the same material,' said the fawn. 'Even though our skin and colour are different, our flesh is the same. Think about the many ways in which we are alike.' The hunter was persuaded by the fawn and regretted killing the deer. He took the fawn home with him and looked after her. And through the years the deer showed him more love than his own children did. When the deer was fully grown he took her to the forest and gave her back her freedom.

Bawa wrote that everyone who heard the story cried. They thought about the animals they themselves had eaten, and said: 'We realise now that we had no compassion or wisdom.'[76]

The reason I am writing about nonviolence when the heading of this chapter is compassion is because I believe they are strongly linked. To be able to open ourselves up totally to the power of compassion we need to embrace *ahimsa*. Compassion can flow from taking a stand for the other's right to live his or her own life, and live a decent life. A precondition for violence is *not* identifying ourselves with the other, not feeling empathy for their situation and suffering. When you practise compassion you take the opposite direction. In other words, you strive to open your heart to the other as much as possible and you try to include as many beings as possible in this sphere of compassion.

I am reminded of an acquaintance, a woman who has been for me an example of all-embracing compassion. Her job is to look after injured wild birds and animals. Some years ago she looked after five hens. They had come from a factory farm and all their life had been shut in crowded cages with no possibility of moving about naturally. Over time she got to know these hens as individuals. One was shy and stood on the sidelines, another sought out human company and liked its neck stroked. When I spoke to this woman a few months ago she sounded distressed. The previous day one of the hens had died in her arms. 'Her body shuddered and I saw how her gaze turned inwards,' she told me. She had tried heart massage but it hadn't helped.

I was touched by the tenderness in the woman's voice. Think what the human heart is capable of. A hen, a small creature worth very little in the human world; in fact, many of us see hens mainly as egg-producing machines. But this woman's heart was wide open to the hens. She felt what they felt and suffered with them. For her, they were valuable creatures.

Is compassion a biblical concept? The Old Testament contains several words in Hebrew which can be translated as compassion or sympathy. *Rachamim* is the most common. The word's root, *rechem*, means womb and suggests our compassion should be as unconditional as that of a mother for her child. In Jewish services God is often called 'the compassionate One' and 'Father of compassion', and Jews are encouraged to live a life of compassion. In a Christian context compassion has often been diminished to mean pity, feeling sorry for someone, but that definition misses that the concept is about action as well as feelings. The person you feel for, you try to help. A Latin American liberation theologian says of biblical compassion that 'it is single-minded engagement with the weak, the poor and the oppressed. It guards their rights; it is identical to an absolute sense of justice.'[77]

Compassion is, then, a stance which the Jewish-Christian tradition regards as fundamental. Mechthild writes:

> *'When are we like God? I will tell you.*
> *In so far as we love compassion and practise it steadfastly,*
> *to that extent do we resemble the heavenly Creator*
> *who practises these things ceaselessly in us.'[78]*

Mechthild is saying something important. Compassion is God's, just as love is God's. It is something we discover, enter into, set free inside ourselves. We can practise this – opening up to compassion – but the reality of compassion is a part of God's reality and nothing we can achieve on our own.

A compassionate diet

In the story of the creation, God indicated a vegetarian diet for humans and animals. This fact has led many Christians, especially those in the Orthodox Church, to see vegetarianism as an ideal to strive for. During a journey in Egypt a friend of mine, Tomas Einarsson, asked a Coptic bishop why people of his faith avoided animal products during Lent. 'We eat this special food because we want to live in the way God wanted us to live in the beginning,' he answered. 'Lent is a time for spiritual awareness, so we try to avoid food which is an obvious result of the Fall. When we do this we get a taste of the food served in Paradise.'[79]

People choose to eat vegetarian food for many reasons, including health and environmental considerations. In this exercise, however, the emphasis is on vegetarianism as an expression of compassion. The less meat and other animal products we buy, the fewer animals have to live miserable lives in factory farms.

Exercise
Vegetarian meals

- Try to let as many meals as possible be vegetarian. When you shop for them, prepare them and eat them, be happy that you are in a concrete way practising compassion. You can say to yourself: 'No one has had to die so that I could have this meal.'

'What is a heart filled with compassion? It is a heart on fire for the whole of creation: for people, for the birds, for all animals, for the demons and all beings that exist.'[80]

Isaac of Syria

Kindness

People's everyday signs of affection are beautiful. That was something I rediscovered after a few months in a British jail. Someone rests a hand on your shoulder, gives you a hug. There weren't many such gestures in prison.

There are many ways to express compassion in daily life and when we are 'walking the spiritual path' we try to make the most of these opportunities. Kindness is, I feel, one of the concrete ways of expressing compassion. Kindness has a lot to do with thoughtfulness and it is possible to behave thoughtfully even when we don't feel like that inside. I can smile at someone even though I'm in a bad mood. Through our own actions we can affect our whole person: our feelings, thoughts, and so on.

Exercise
Kindness

- Be generous with your company, your time and your money. Encourage someone if they seem to be tired. Try to help others in any way you can.

The expanding circle of compassion

Often it isn't hard to sympathise and stretch out a hand to people and animals we know and like, but if we want to practise our capacity for compassion we have to reach out to others too – to strangers, people we find difficult, aggressive youngsters, animals that aren't the slightest bit cute, and so on. This process can be compared to the historical development usually known as 'the expanding circle of compassion'. Through the centuries there has been a gradual development of moral concern and people have come to understand that our circle of compassion has to be widened to include many more. The circle has expanded from consisting of our own tribes to including the nation and eventually the whole of humanity. Different groups have been taken into the circle at different times. White westerners did not regard black people as equals until some time into the last century. Homosexuals have until recently risked capital punishment – and still do, in some countries – if they are publicly open about their love.

Exercise
Expanding the circle

- What does your circle of compassion look like? Who are those standing on the outside?

- Be aware of the suffering, worry and anxiety of others. Don't give in to the spontaneous reaction to back off, to turn away. Identify yourself with the other, but temporarily, because you can't take on another's suffering. If possible, ask whether you can help. Otherwise do what you can to help the other being out of trouble.

'Remember those in prison as if you were their fellow prisoners, and those who are ill-treated as if you yourselves were suffering.'

Hebrews 13:3 (NIV)

Practising humility

> *'Around humility God gathered all the virtues.'*[81]
>
> Hildegard of Bingen

Humility can mean many things. At times the word has been used to stifle people's self-confidence and creative power, but correctly interpreted I think humility means finding your proper place in life. Knowing that you are wonderfully made but not the centre of the universe. I am a piece of a puzzle and I fit in, among many others. So, how do I relate properly to the world around me? On a personal level there are many aspects, such as those mentioned in the exercises below. For me, the question of humility for humankind as a community is an important one.

Humanity has major problems with its self-image. For a long time we have told ourselves that we are creation's crown. Naturally *we* are the most important thing God created, or so we think. There are many of us today who have begun to realise that this approach is problematical, but it's not easy to climb down from the pedestal. We find it hard to believe that other creatures and objects have an intrinsic value in God's eyes. Can it be true that a monkey's playfulness and the song of a cricket make God happy?

As Christians we believe that humankind has a special

function: to have dominion over animals and nature, as God's representative. We can read about this in the book of Genesis. A warped interpretation of these verses might be: 'Everything that benefits humankind is permitted and right.' But what does it mean to have dominion over someone? It depends how we view power. Power provides the opportunity to take responsibility for others. Power means having the resources to help and sustain – or destroy – others. Which way shall we choose?

Humble people seldom put themselves and their needs in the centre, unless they are important needs. Couldn't it be that way with a humble humanity? At the very least we could start by not destroying the environment or taking the life of other creatures, except in cases of vital need. Think how much would change.

Our relationship with animals and nature has seldom been included in the traditional definition of humility, which says a lot in itself. I don't mean it is always easy to apply this virtue in all relationships. Sometimes opposing interests are involved and that makes decision-making difficult, but in our relationship to other sentient creatures I wish we could have the same attitude as the 18th-century Quaker Joshua Evans: 'Since we cannot give life, let us be careful not to take it.'[82]

Acting in this spirit, one intention I might adopt could be to ensure that my life does not impinge on the life of others. I do not want my life to be built on others' suffering, and I will do what I can to avoid that.

The Benedictine tradition

One summer a number of years ago I lived in a Christian community in Duluth, Minnesota. We opened our door to the homeless, campaigned against military recruiting methods, organised demonstrations against nuclear weapons, and so on. Every Thursday we went to the morning mass at McCabe's, a retreat run by Benedictine nuns. We sat in a circle, and after a short sermon given by a priest we could all share our thoughts about the texts of the day. Sister Lois usually had observations to make, in her clear, calm voice, and I always appreciated her comments, which were often as comprehensive as the priest's. After mass we used to have coffee and chat for a while. I remember that Sister Lois made no secret of the fact that she wished there could be women priests in the Catholic Church. For me she was a reminder that humility is not about belittling yourself.

When Saint Benedict wrote his rule in the sixth century, the chapter on humility became one of the longest. This rule still forms the basis of the monastic life in all Benedictine communities throughout the world. The people Benedict's rule were written for – men in the Roman Empire – lived in a culture that had values similar to those of the western world today. Qualities such as conventional manliness, power and independence were highly esteemed. The humility that Benedict wanted the brothers in his order to practise was naturally the complete opposite to those ideals. Benedict saw pride as humankind's greatest weakness. As we have seen, this is perhaps more true of men than women, but I believe we women are not immune from the ideals of our time: being upwardly mobile, working on ourselves as individuals so that *I* will become stronger and achieve more.

Benedict challenges us to take twelve steps to become more humble. In the language of today they might read something like this:[83]

- Recognise the presence of God in your life.
- Accept God's will.
- Accept spiritual guidance.
- Persevere – don't give up the struggle.
- Admit your faults and mistakes.
- Live simply.
- Be honest about yourself.
- Be willing to learn from others.
- Listen to others.
- Speak kindly to others.
- Accept others as they are.
- Be calm and in the present.

Exercise
Practising humility

- Do you want to practise humility according to Benedict's model? Make up your mind to practise one step a week, over a twelve-week period, starting with the first one. Write the week's theme on a slip of paper and put it in a prominent place. Don't throw away the old notes but try to bear the previous weeks' themes in mind. If you would like to know more about the rule of St Benedict, see the reading tips at the back of this book. Obviously it takes a lifetime to practise it all, but having this path of humility as a focus in life for a few months is a good start.

Gratitude

After a summer in Paraguay, when I washed all my laundry by hand, I saw washing machines in a completely new light. How much easier they make our lives! Then gradually I lost that feeling. And that's the way it is, unfortunately; we become unavoidably accustomed to the standard we enjoy. I have no idea what the solution could be but I try to remind myself often how privileged I am.

Our ability to feel gratitude has a fundamental effect on our approach to life. Practise gratitude and you automatically promote humility. Why is that so? Being grateful is one way to see and admit your need for others and for 'the provider of all things', God. We have been given life itself as a gift, the greatest gift of all. Don't let us take that for granted.

Exercise
Gratitude

- Give thanks for the things you experience, the people you meet, the beautiful things you see, tricky situations which taught you something; for a night's sleep, for the clear air after a shower of rain. Try to discover all the ways in which you have been blessed.

- Don't be afraid to express thanks to others for what you have received from them.

- Don't compare yourself with others, for what they own or what they achieve. You won't benefit from it and it stops you feeling thankful for your own life.

Simplicity

I learned something about simplicity from two women I got to know through my work as a deacon. We had started a weekly soup lunch in the area where they lived. One day when we met up they were distraught about the earthquake in Pakistan and all the people who had been made homeless just as the cold winter was approaching. They demanded that I find out how we could help the people affected and the following week they turned up with big bags full of clothes that they wanted to give to the victims of the earthquake. They were poorly off themselves but now there were others whose need for clothes was greater.

Simplicity is about having the right approach to material things, to be able to enjoy them and use them without being owned by them. There is an inside and an outside to simplicity: my attitude and my material circumstances.

Greed is the opposite pole to humility. Greed means enlarging my living space at others' expense – my environmental space, for example (meaning the use of natural resources and the environmental pollution that is acceptable without impairing the ability of future generations to support themselves and sustain biological diversity). That is why simplicity and humility go together.

Striving for a simple lifestyle also goes hand in hand with gratitude. When you don't demand a high standard of living, it is easier to feel gratitude for what you have, and by cultivating gratitude it is easier to get rid of unnecessary – or what you discover to be unnecessary – objects and desires.

Exercise
Simplicity

- Give up something you appreciate but which you know someone else would be happy to have.

- Make it a regular habit to give away things you no longer use.

'If your brothers are planning great building projects, turn it into something holy and say: "Oh, dearly beloved brothers, let us build the Holy Trinity a delightful palace in our souls with the Holy Scripture as the timber and with noble virtues as the stones."'

Mechthild of Magdeburg[84]

Our impact on the environment

An ecological footprint is the area of land needed to produce the resources an individual consumes and to handle the waste generated. For a sustainable future this area should not be more than 1.8 hectares per person. Today, the average ecological footprint of each person living in the UK is 5.45 global hectares. Important factors are air travel, use of cars, heating our homes and food habits.

Someone with a small ecological footprint is probably responsible for emitting a low quantity of greenhouse gases, but ecological footprint is a wider concept than effect on the climate alone. Other kinds of environmental impact are also included in the footprint.

Exercise
Reducing our footprint

- Go to www.myfootprint.org to calculate the effect your life has on the environment. Then decide to make one concrete effort to reduce your footprint. If you would rather read about it, I suggest *The Food Revolution* by John Robbins, to get an idea of how your eating habits affect the environment and the climate.

'God desires that all the world be pure in his sight.
The earth should not be injured.
The earth should not be destroyed.'[85]

Hildegard of Bingen

About the night

It was after we had moved to Styal, the new prison for women. There the cells were arranged on three floors around a large atrium. Every sound was magnified in the huge building. I was woken in the middle of the night by a scream that tore right through my body. At first I thought it was an animal, but of course there weren't any in the prison. It had to be one of the other women. The screams continued, as if the person was in terrible pain. Tears came to my eyes; I felt so powerless. Otherwise it was silent. Why did none of the guards go to help her? After a long time I heard footsteps and the jangling of keys. I had no idea what had happened and could see nothing through my cell's little window, but eventually it went quiet.

The following day I heard that it was Susan, five months pregnant, who had suffered a miscarriage. For some reason the warders had taken over half an hour to get to her. What kind of godforsaken place is this, I thought, where such things can happen? How can we allow a prison system that deprives the inmates of dignity and treats them as an inferior kind of human being? I had been aware myself of how I was affected by the particular way the prison warders looked at me, or rather looked through me. If you were feeling low it would definitely make you even more depressed.

God, when are we going to learn compassion? When will it be allowed to include everyone?

John of the Cross, a 16th-century Spanish Carmelite friar, coined the phrase *the dark night of the soul*. Actually, he wrote about two different nights on the spiritual journey, those of the soul and the spirit. During the night of the soul, the spiritual life offers no comfort; it feels empty and dark and it is hard to pray. The things that stand in the way of our being open to God, such as a feeling that we are good at praying and other ego-centred attitudes, will wither away. That is how many interpret what takes place in the night. The night of the spirit goes deeper: there is a fear of having lost your faith; you doubt everything.

Are there other kinds of existential night that men and women today struggle with? We have already seen one example in the chapter about the dark night of the feminine. Another darkness that can affect those who are working for a better world is hopelessness. Any advances made seem so small. The opposition is too massive. We'll never reach our goal! Apart from the fact that hopelessness is a heavy burden for us to bear, there is also the risk that we will put up a barrier to avoid feeling the pain, and in doing so shut off our emotions. This is when we need each other and all the available resources: time for tranquillity and rest, people who will listen and understand, new creative forms of engagement.

The night of the soul can also be about feelings of meaninglessness, or despair when you are faced with your own and others' faults. All these feelings need to be recognised. The only way forward is to live through them. It is a great help if you can find someone with whom to share your thoughts and feelings. Also, be kind to yourself. Know that what you are trying to do for others is very valuable in God's eyes.

Another aspect of the night, which is also prominent in the texts of the mystics, is about being emptied. We are so easily filled up – with concern about our lives, anxiety and so on – that there is no room for anything new to be born within us. Inner emptiness is not a goal in itself; the aim of emptiness is to be filled. According to the mystics we can facilitate the birth of God within us by letting go of our selfishness and our involvement with … well, with what?

Sometimes it is difficult to understand the mystics' writings, such as when we are told to let go of worldly things. Instinctively, I protest, 'That can't be right! God doesn't want us to turn our back on the world.' But how are we to understand what they have written? I see two ways of doing this.

One is to explore whether 'earthly' means what we think it means. Maybe they mean what we would call worldly cares, such as wealth, status, pride, and so on. In that case it is easier to understand.

The second possibility is quite simply to admit that they

were influenced by neoplatonism with its hierarchy, where the spiritual is superior to the worldly and much more important. We know better today. We have understood that God is involved in earthly matters and that we should be, too.

One theologian who has contemplated the concept of emptiness is Dorothee Sölle. She has asked herself what it is in today's society that we particularly need to let go of. She concluded that three things, three forces, keep us imprisoned: the ego, possessions and violence.

The ego. Letting go of the ego means not being wrapped up in myself. Only then can I really take in the beauty that surrounds me and the suffering of our fellow beings. This presupposes that I feel secure in myself. I know from experience the burden of self-consciousness. When I was growing up I sometimes suffered from shyness. It felt as if I were imprisoned within myself. But when you have reached the stage of having found yourself and liking yourself, that's the time to face the world.

Today the ego is connected to material things, writes Sölle. We are encouraged to accumulate possessions, which means we need to look after and protect what we have. That takes time and energy. To be ego-obsessed can also be about the need to retain or raise our status in society.

In the struggle against egocentricity we find support in the spirituality of the mystics. We can let ourselves go, and cast ourselves into God's arms and into working for others. We do not need to be our own gods. There is someone to 'lose yourself in'. As Simone Weil (1909-1943), French philosopher and mystic, wrote: 'Why should I be worried? It is not up to me to think about myself. It is up to me to think about God. And it is up to God to think about me.'[86]

Possessions. As we have seen, our culture is extremely concerned with material things: new products and the status that results from outer attributes. One problematic aspect among many is that our attitude towards objects can influence our attitude to people, animals and nature. We want to own and control. The philosopher Descartes stated in the 17th century that the duty of humanity is to be the master and owner of nature. Today we can see where this approach has led us. We have just about reached the limit of what the planet can cope with.

We need to learn to recognise the real needs among all the created ones. What material things do I need to let go of?

Violence. No one likes the thought of violence. Those who propagate the use of violence often speak instead in terms of defence, security, peacekeeping and similar concepts. What this 'power' demands is only our obedience, that we are passive, neutral bystanders and that we continue to believe in the credo 'weapons mean security'. Violence against others means that we see ourselves as separate from them: 'He has nothing to do with me.' Here the mystics' experience of the oneness of all can help us.

It is this emptiness, this poverty, that God wants from us, maintains Sölle: that we abandon our present attitude of worshipping ego, possessions and violence. In different ways these are all about control and ownership. We need to practise letting go, in big things and small.

In several places in the New Testament Christians are described as strangers in the world. They live among the 'heathen' who cannot understand what the Christian life is all about. Christians live according to other values and have other goals in life than do the people around them. Today it is often difficult to work out what could be meant by Christian 'estrangement' when we seem to be very much at home in society and culture. I think Sölle's premise is a powerful interpretation of what estrangment from the world could mean in our culture.[87]

Exercise

Acknowledging sorrow

Not everything on this earth is beautiful, not everything causes us to react with wonder. There are forces, internal and external, that are destructive. This next exercise is about accepting the sorrow and pain we feel when we see human beings, animals and nature being damaged or destroyed. We may feel sorrow, too, for people who let themselves be driven to destructive behaviour (and sometimes that is us). We see that this harm also affects God, who suffers along with all those who are in distress. Let us allow our feelings to be a part of God's sorrow, which is born of the great tenderness and love God has for creation.

- When you see terrible things on TV or read about them in the paper, allow your sorrow to rise up inside you, release it, and cry.

A mysticism for all

There are many ways to define inner growth. Teresa of Avila described the mystical process as a journey between different rooms in an inner castle. I tried to read her books during a period when I threw myself enthusiastically into my prayer life, but despite my good intentions I found it hard to benefit from her experiences and advice. It was so far removed from my own prayers, my own life.

The 'classical' mystical process is usually expressed as three steps: purification, enlightenment and union. Purification involves combating the ego through prayer, fasting and other methods, thereby gaining control over your desires and turning completely to God. Enlightenment means being reformed in your inner self by Christ – becoming like Christ, in fact. The final stage takes place when the old self has disappeared completely and there is a blissful union with God.

There are at least two problems with this approach.

Firstly, it doesn't start with what is good – God's good creation and grace – but with our 'fall', our disengagement from God. Instead, the starting point ought to be gratitude and joy in life, and then we can move on to how we fail in our response to God's overflowing love.

Secondly, the classical spiritual journey ends with the individual's joyful union with God, but it is not made sufficiently clear that love for God and love for the world are inseparable.

I would like to give an outline of an 'ordinary person's mystical process', taking these two arguments into consideration. Others have made similar attempts: my basic structure has been inspired by Matthew Fox, an American priest and frontline figure within what is called Creation Spirituality.[88]

The basic premise comprises four aspects of life: feeling joy, serving, sinking and being reborn. The first three aspects correspond to the first three chapters of this book.

Feeling joy – enjoying life and the beauty of creation – is linked to *God in creation*.

Serving – feeling compassion for every living thing and defending people, animals and nature against threats – has been discussed in *God in engagement*.

Sinking – accepting life's burdens – is discussed in the chapter *About the night*.

These three paths are integrated in the fourth aspect, being reborn. The first three have no specific chronological order but 'being reborn' has to be the final step because this process builds on the experiences gained from feeling joy, serving and sinking into darkness.

I believe most people go through these stages at some time in their life. By consciously reflecting on them we can become more deeply involved in these ways of experiencing reality. My starting point is that the spiritual life is woven in with the rest of our life. God is concerned with life in its entirety, and so is mysticism. The very heart of this view of mysticism is that one should exist in the present and be open to reality – because God is present in what really is: in beauty and oneness, but also in pain over beauty made ugly, as well as in the fight to realise oneness, tear down walls and build a better world.

Mechthild of Magdeburg will contribute her thoughts in the following section.

Feeling joy

We discover the beauty of life over and over again. Our experience of creation is intensified by practising presence and wonder. We feel gratitude for all the beauty and complexity that is creation around us. More and more appears as holy to us: the goodness of ordinary people, a moment of silence during a walk through the woods, the loyalty my dog shows me. We appreciate and enjoy all that we have for free – it is the antidote to the frenzy of consumerism. (To say that we are content with what we have is rather revolutionary today. The forces that encourage us continually to consume more and more would call it dangerous.)

Mechthild tells how she hears God emphasise his presence in creation: 'God says: Now is the time to tell you where I am and where I will be. I am in Myself, in all places in all things as I ever have been without beginning.'[89]

Serving

I think the word *serve* is beautiful. I think about Jesus and how he turned all hierarchical ideas upside down when he said power should be expressed through serving. However, it is also a term that has been abused. Its meaning is no longer interpreted as anti-hierarchical but implies instead that those at the bottom of the social pile should make life easier for those at the top. I want to reclaim this word, and feel that care and prophetic engagement together make up the right definition of service in the world. This is the mystical life put into practice.

The combination is important: compassion for all and working for justice. Naturally, as individuals we have to choose what we want to get involved in – we can't all fight every battle – but we must not lose sight of these two aspects. Care is about individuals who are suffering here and now, and how we can help them. Working for justice concerns the structures in our society which need to be changed so that no living creature will ever again have to suffer violence and oppression. It's about opposition to the forces in the world which cause death and destruction. It's about creating the good society.

In this our work we share God's own life, which is one of love flowing out towards creation. 'When we on earth pour out compassion and mercy from the depths of our hearts,' writes Mechtild, 'and give to the poor and dedicate our bodies to the service of the broken, to that very extent do we resemble the Holy Spirit who is a compassionate out-pouring of the Creator and the Son.'[90]

Sinking

Mechthild often speaks about sinking, about 'descending' into feelings and experiences which are heavy and where God seems absent. We should not suppress this part of reality: 'Whoever at some point is seriously wounded by true love will never become healthy again unless he kisses that same mouth by which his soul was wounded.'[91]

Embracing the difficult experiences of our various 'nights' and learning everything we can from them makes it possible for us to find new hope. Eventually the dawn will break.

Being reborn

By trusting in God's loving presence and through the openness/ emptiness the Night has created within us, something new is born. Actually, it isn't new: the divine has existed within us all along, but now it can illuminate our life in a new way. The mystics call this 'God's birth within us'. In mystic literature it is described as a one-off event, a breakthrough, but I believe we all experience moments of this from time to time. Sometimes we just find ourselves there: self-consciousness has gone, care for others has taken over our soul and we reach out, our creativity flowing.

Mechthild describes how God's outpouring love can fill the whole person. When this happens, the love flows through us and out into the world. 'Great is the overflow of Divine Love for it is never still. Always ceaselessly and tirelessly it pours itself out, so that the small vessel which is ourselves might be filled to the brim and might also overflow.'

What we hope for is that these moments will be more frequent and last longer as we follow this mystical path of engagement in life.

A year's programme

Naturally you can use the exercises in this book in any way
you choose – or not at all. You can select those that seem relevant for your own life and ignore the others, but for those
who are serious about practising spirituality in this way and
would appreciate some structure, here is a programme to
follow. It is spread over one year and divided into six different
periods. Each one of these periods is based on a theme taken
from the chapter *God in Creation*, in which the joy of life is
central, plus two different themes from the chapter *God in
Engagement*. In this way both these aspects of life – experiencing joy and serving – are included throughout the year.

Months one and two:
Being in the present, simplifying my existence and reflecting
on how I can live a more environmentally friendly life.

    Conscious presence, page 73.

    Simplicity, page 135.

    Reducing our footprint, page 136.

Months three and four:
Joy at being God's dwelling place, practising showing kindness, and noticing individuals I'm not normally aware of.

    The inner sanctuary, page 48.

Kindness, page 123.
Expanding the circle, page 125.

Months five and six:

Allowing myself to be touched by the wonder of creation, turning my back on the frenzy of consumerism and practising Benedictine humility. (The last exercise is actually spread over twelve weeks but it can be shortened by focusing on each theme for five days.)

Wonder, page 75.
Liberate yourself from the prison, page 115.
Practising humility, page 131.

Months seven and eight:

Treating everything and everyone with reverence, striving to adopt a vegetarian diet, and developing my feelings of gratitude.

Reverence, page 78.
Vegetarian meals, page 122.
Gratitude, page 132.

Months nine and ten:

Regarding all living things as part of one and the same whole, accepting the sorrow that comes from seeing the destructiveness in the world, and practising using anger at injustice in a constructive way.

Connectedness, page 86.
Acknowledging sorrow, page 145.
Anger, page 110.

Months eleven and twelve:
Allowing my emotions to empower my life and work, and practising intervention in destructive situations.

Passion, page 83.
Intervention, page 113.

Conclusion

Historically, churches have often been sceptical about mystics. Bishops and priests have felt threatened by accounts of direct contact with the divine. It has also been a class issue. What will happen if God speaks directly to people in the lower levels of society and empowers them?

Constance Fitzgerald, a prioress in an American Carmelite convent, sees a connection between the oppression of mysticism and the oppression of women. She says that the end of the 17th century was a breaking point, when movements based on contemplation, such as the Quietists, were banned, and the mystical experiences of women were silenced. 'Have no doubt,' she writes, 'that the muting of contemplation was/is directly related to the place of women in society, the role of conscience in religion and politics, the fear of direct inspiration of the Spirit, and the transformative and therefore seditious character of contemplative prayer.'[93]

If her theory is true it is both disturbing and intriguing. Can this development have been influenced in some way by the changed world view we looked at in the chapter *God in Creation*? I believe so. Often considered to be closely connected to the earth, women suffered when creation lost its indwelling holiness in the perceptions of the Church. Once reason had become the highest ideal, no one any longer paid attention to the visions of uneducated women. It is to be hoped that the tide has turned again today, so that all people – men and women – who want to hear the still voice of God in themselves and in the world, and who value wonderment and reverence for creation, are taken seriously. The increasing interest in retreats and meditation is heartwarming. We need more silence in our churches, but the fullness of the contemplative approach will only be attained when it is combined with a mystical ethic and involvement in the world.

Let us hope that churches today are prepared to be open to mystical spirituality. This might involve courses in Christian meditation, study groups about the creation-positive mystics, or action to protect living creatures and the environment from destruction. The knowledge of God's presence at the heart of every created thing and a reverence for life in all its forms could be the keynotes of renewal.

It is six o'clock and already dark outside. Pelle has made lentil soup and is taking warm bread out of the oven. We sink down onto our chairs, all four of us, with a communal sigh; now it's time to wind down. A candle is alight on the table. We take hold of each other's hands for a short moment of silence. While we eat we share the events of the day with each other. There is no hurry; each person can have as long as they like and no one is interrupted.

For the past year I have had my home in a community

where we live and work together. I often think of the help the others have been to me and how we are so much stronger together. We have different paths to follow and sometimes they merge. The possibility of living as 'mystics in the world' is opened up by the encouragement, as well as the challenges, we offer each other. Not everyone can live in a community but I wish everyone could have some kind of fellowship to support them in their attempt to live an impassioned, involved life. Perhaps for some people their church congregation is such a community, in which case that's fantastic. Others look in vain for this kind of spirituality in their church and that's when you have to look somewhere else instead.

It is not a question of trying to appear righteous before God, with the right belief or action. There is another way and that is to open yourself to the Holy Spirit and allow her to renew your life. It is only because God's Spirit inspires and strengthens us that we are able to choose the mystic path.

Love challenges us to go further, one step at a time.

'The divine heart resembles red gold burning in a great fire of coals. He places her [the soul] into his glowing heart.'

Mechthild of Magdeburg[94]

Helpful books and websites

God within us

The book by Lavinia Byrne that inspired me some ten years ago is called *Woman at the Altar: The Ordination of Women in the Roman Catholic Church* and was published in 1994. Werner Jeanrond's book *Call and Response* was published in English in 1997 by Continuum Publishing Group.

Carol Flinders is an American author and lecturer who has discovered a spirituality which satisfies both her spiritual hunger and her feminist thirst. She is inspired not only by Christian but also Hindu mystics. The book about her own journey is called *At the Root of this Longing: Reconciling a Spiritual Hunger and a Feminist Thirst*. Some years earlier she wrote *Enduring Grace: Living Portraits of Seven Women Mystics,* about mystics in the Christian faith who had inspired her.

Dorothee Sölle's *The Silent Cry: Mysticism and Resistance* is a book with a mission similar to this one: to explore and develop the connection between a mystical way of looking at the world and involvement for the sake of the world.

She Who Is: The Mystery of God in Feminist Theological Discourse is a book I can recommend as one of the canons of feminist theology, assuming the reader has a basic grasp of theology. The author is Elizabeth A. Johnson, a Catholic professor of theology. The book is mainly about God as triune.

God in creation

She Who Changes, by Carol P. Christ, covers all the important aspects of process theology in a comprehensible form. Christ compares this theology, or rather philosophy, with different types of feminist theology and argues that the process perspective resolves several of the conflicts that exist between the various theologies.

Christ in All Things, by Ursula King, is a study of Pierre Teilhard de Chardin's spirituality and its importance for us today. Among other things King discusses Teilhard's understanding of interreligious dialogue and spirituality which has its roots in the third world.

There are several books available which try to explain the meaning of the new discoveries in physics. One is *The Elegant Universe* by Brian Greene, a relatively easy to read book, included in the bibliography below.

God in engagement

The Ploughshares (or Plowshares) Movement takes its name from the prophet Isaiah's vision that swords will be turned into ploughshares (a part of the plough). The movement started in the US in 1980 and came to the UK ten years later. Information about the movement can be found on the website www.plowshares.se/english

The Ecumenical Accompaniment Programme in Palestine and Israel, EAPPI, is run by the World Council of Churches. In Britain the co-ordination of the programme is a joint project of members of Churches Together in Britain and Ireland and Christian Aid, implemented and managed by Quaker Peace & Social Witness. Go to www.eappi.org for more information.

Two organisations working with justice issues:
Amnesty International www.amnesty.org.uk
Church Action on Poverty www.church-poverty.org.uk

Regarding peace work, in addition to those mentioned below, you can find contact details of many organisations by visiting the website of the Network of Christian Peace Organisations at www.ncpo.org.uk
Trident Ploughshares www.tridentploughshares.org
Campaign Against the Arms Trade www.caat.org.uk
CND www.cnduk.org
Peace News www.peacenews.info
Network for Peace www.networkforpeace.org.uk
War Resisters International www.wri-irg.org
Scotland's for Peace www.scotland4peace.org

There are many organisations and websites dealing with anti-consumerism. One in the US is the Simple Living Network (www.simpleliving.net). Adbusters (www.adbusters.org) is another network of people concerned about the erosion of our physical and cultural environment by commercial forces.

On the subject of animal theology Pelle Strindlund and I have written *Every Creature a Word of God: Compassion for Animals as Christian Spirituality* published by Vegetarian Advocates Press in 2008. An association formed in the US to encourage Christians to become vegetarians is the Christian Vegetarian Association www.christianveg.com. CVA in the UK was established in 2004, see www.cvauk.homecall.co.uk.

Joan Chittister, a Benedictine nun from the US, has written many books on the subject of Christian spirituality today. *Twelve Steps to Inner Freedom* is a short book about humility based on the rule of Saint Benedict. In *Wisdom Distilled from the Daily* Chittister discusses several aspects of Benedictine spirituality. It is easy to read and very engaging.

Bibliography

Teresa av Avila (1974). *Den inre borgen.* Helsingborg: Karmeliterna.

Hildegard av Bingen (1997). *Hildegard av Bingen: Hennes liv – hennes verk.* Stockholm: Cordia.

Bischofberger, Erwin och Eklöf, Christel (1986). *Guds födelse i människan: Om mystik och inre bön i kristen tradition.* Delsbo: Bokförlaget Åsak.

Chittister, Joan (2003). *Twelve Steps to Inner Freedom: Humility Revisited.* Erie: Benetvision.

Christ, Carol P. (2003). *She Who Changes: Re-Imagining the Divine in the World.* New York: Palgrave Macmillan.

Cooper, Tim (1990). *Green Christianity: Caring for the Whole Creation.* London: Spire.

Danielsson, Ulf (2004). *Stjärnor och äpplen som faller: En bok om upptäckter och märkvärdigheter i universum.* Stockholm: Månpocket.

Davies, Paul (1989). *The Cosmic Blueprint: New Discoveries in Nature's Creative Ability to Order the Universe.* Pocket Books.

De Mello, Anthony (1987). *Sadhana: A Way to God.* Anand: Gujarat Sahitya Prakash.

Dreyer, Elizabeth (2005). *Passionate Spirituality: Hildegard of Bingen and Hadewijch of Brabant.* New York: Paulist Press.

Dutton, Elisabeth (2008). *A Revelation of Love.* Plymouth: Rowman & Littlefield Publishers.

Edman, Stefan (2006). *Förundran: Tankar om vår stund på jorden.* Stockholm: Cordia.

Einarsson, Tomas (2005). *Paradiset åter: Vegetarianism och djurrätt i kristen tro och tradition.* Skellefteå: Artos.

Einhorn, Stefan (1998). *En dold Gud: Om religion, vetenskap och att söka Gud.* Stockholm: Bokförlaget Forum.

Fox, Matthew (1972). *On Becoming a Musical, Mystical Bear.* Mahwah: Paulist Press.

— (1988). *The Coming of the Cosmic Christ: The Healing of Mother Earth and the Birth of a Global Renaissance.* San Francisco: Harper & Row.

— (1982). *Meditations with Meister Eckhart.* Santa Fe: Bear & Company Publishing.

— (1990). *A Spirituality Named Compassion.* San Francisco: Harper & Row.

— (1991). *Creation Spirituality: Liberating Gifts for the Peoples of the Earth.* New York: HarperCollins Publishers.

Gallagher, Blanche (1988). *Meditations with Teilhard de Chardin.* Santa Fe: Bear & Company Publishing.

Geels, Antoon (2000). *Kristen mystik: Ur psykologisk synvinkel.* Del 1. Skellefteå: Norma bokförlag.

Gilbert, Joan (1986). 'Joshua Evans: Consistent Quaker', in *The Friendly Vegetarian,* No 13, Spring 1986. www.vegetarian-friends.net/issue6.html#7

Greene, Brian (1999). *The Elegant Universe: Superstrings, Hidden*

Dimensions and the Quest for the Ulitimate Theory. New York: WW Norton.

Grey, Mary C. (1997). *Prophecy and Mysticism: The Heart of the Postmodern Church*. Edinburgh: T&T Clark.

Jansdotter, Maria (2003). *Ekofeminism i teologin: Genusuppfattning, natursyn och gudsuppfattning hos Anne Primavesi, Catherine Keller och Carol Christ*. Karlstad: Karlstad University Press.

Johnston, William (2002). *Upplyst av kärlek: En handledning i kristen bön och djupmeditation*. Stockholm: Veritas.

King, Ursula (1997). *Christ in All Things: Exploring Spirituality with Teilhard de Chardin*. London: SCM Press.

Lanzetta, Beverly J. (2005). *Radical Wisdom: A Feminist Mystical Theology*. Minneapolis: Fortress Press.

Mechthild of Magdeburg (1998 [written between 1250 and 1270]). *The Flowing Light of the Godhead*. New York: Paulist Press.

McFague, Sallie (1993). *The Body of God: An Ecological Theology*. Minneapolis: Fortress Press.

Nadeau, Robert and Kafatos, Menas (1999). *The Non-Local Universe: The New Physics and Matters of the Mind*. New York: Oxford University Press.

Julian of Norwich (2008 [written at the end of the 14th century]). *A Revelation of Love*. Plymouth, USA: Rowman & Littlefield Publishers. (Introduced, edited and modernised by Elisabeth Dutton.)

Radford Ruether, Rosemary (2002). *Visionary Women: Three Medieval Mystics*. Minneapolis: Fortress Press.

Sölle, Dorothee (2001). *The Silent Cry: Mysticism and Resistance.* Minneapolis: Fortress Press.

Stenström, Hanna, ed. (1992). *Kan vi tro på Gud Fader?* Uppsala: Svenska kyrkans forskningsråd.

Stinissen, Wilfrid (1990). *En bok om kristen djupmeditation.* Örebro: Libris.

Isaac the Syrian (2001). *Landet där tankarna funnit ro/Isak Syriern.* Sturefors: Silentium.

Teilhard de Chardin, Pierre (1978). *The Heart of Matter.* London: Collins.

Toolan, David (2001). *At Home in the Cosmos.* New York: Orbis Books.

Uhlein, Gabriele (1983). *Meditations with Hildegard of Bingen.* Santa Fe: Bear & Company Publishing.

Walters, Kerry S. and Portmess, Lisa, ed. (2001). *Religious Vegetarianism: from Hesiod to the Dalai Lama.* Albany: State University of New York Press.

Weiss, Andrew (2004). *Beginning Mindfulness: Learning the Way of Awareness.* Novato: New World Library.

Woodruff, Sue (1982). *Meditations with Mechtild of Magdeburg.* Santa Fe: Bear & Company Publishing.

Notes

[1] Translation from Anne H King Lenz-Meier 2001, *Hildegard of Bingen: An Integrated Vision*.

[2] One of the authors who helped me discover these mystics is Carol Flinders (see Bibliography).

[3] Woodruff (1982), p 42.

[4] Uhlein (1983), p. 91.

[5] Apart from those in the first part, which are concerned with the relationship to ourselves and God within us.

[6] Fox (1988), p. 38.

[7] Fox (1988), p. 40.

[8] Julian of Norwich (2008), s. 28. Ghostly means supernatural, belonging to spirit rather than matter.

[9] Julian of Norwich (2008), p.80.

[10] 'When Adam fell, so did God's son.' He fell 'into the maiden's womb', down into her human nature and the suffering that was his lot. After his death he fell into hell 'and when he was there he raised up the great root out of the deep depth, which rightfully was joined to him in high heaven'. Julian of Norwich, s. 82-87.

[11] Julian of Norwich (2008), p. 30.

[12] Fox (1982), p. 50.

[13] Julian of Norwich (2008), p.105.

[14] Julian of Norwich (2008), p.103-104.

[15] Mechthild of Magdeburg (1998), p. 71.

[16] Edman (1990), p. 148.

[17] Teresa of Avila, Den inre borgen (The Inner Castle), s. 27–28. It continues 'But if you place a deep black cloth over a crystal through which the sun is shining, it is clear that however much the sun shines, its glow has no effect on the crystal.'

[18] Lanzetta (2005), p. 172.

[19] Woodruff (1982), p. 13f.

[20] Julian of Norwich (2008), p. 113–114.

[21] Mechthild of Magdeburg (1998), p. 325.

[22] Mechthild of Magdeburg (1998), p. 90.

[23] William Johnston, Irish Jesuit living in Tokyo, recommends yoga in *Being in Love: A Practical Guide to Christian Prayer.*

[24] Weiss (2004), pp. 10–11.

[25] De Mello (1987), p. 7 and p. 15.

[26] Julian of Norwich (2008), p. 95.

[27] Inspired by McFague (1993), p. 34.

[28] Colossians I, v.16 and 17.

[29] Danielsson (2003), p. 32.

[30] Edman (2006), p. 66 ff.

[31] Einhorn (1998), p. 127.

[32] Inspired by Nadeau and Kafatos (1999).

[33] Inspired by Christ (2003), p. 63f.

[34] Bischofberger and Eklöf (1986), p. 30f.

[35] Cooper (1990), p. 155.

[36] Julian of Norwich (2008), p.38.

[37] Cooper (1990), p. 154.

[38] Greene (2002), p. 37.

39 Uhlein (1983), p. 49.
40 Fox (1988), p. 121.
41 Fox (1988), p. 129.
42 King (1997), p. 75.
43 King (1997), p. 68.
44 Gallagher (1988), p. 31.
45 King (1997), p. 68.
46 Teilhard (1978), p. 26.
47 Dahlén, (1976), p. 20f.
48 Källstad (1987), p. 81.
49 Julian of Norwich (2008), p. 58 in the Swedish edition.
50 Toolan (2001), chapter eight.
51 Julian of Norwich (2008), p. 28ff.
52 Exercises in conscious presence are inspired by those in *Beginning Mindfulness,* a book by Andrew Weiss which I can recommend.
53 Fox (1982), p. 14.
54 Fox (1982), p. 14.
55 Uhlein (1983), p. 28.
56 Dreyer (2005), p. 43.
57 Geels, p. 174.
58 Dreyer (2005), p. 116-136.
59 Radford Ruether (2002), p. 3.
60 Uhlein (1983), p. 65.
61 Dahlén (1976), p. 21.
62 Uhlein (1983), p. 41.
63 Uhlein (1983), p. 36.

[64] Jeremiah 22:16.
[65] Jansdotter (2003) p. 49.
[66] Hildegard of Bingen (1997), p. 109.
[67] Davies (1990), p. 222.
[68] Julian of Norwich (2008), p. 38.
[69] Chapter 6:12 and 2:2. NIV.
[70] In the Swedish translation, this sentence begins with 'The only thing that God requires from you ...'
A parallel to this Micah text can be found in Matthew chapter 23, verse 23. Jesus is talking to the people and he criticises harshly the Pharisees and those well-read in the scriptures. 'Woe to you, teachers of the law and Pharisees, you hypocrites! You give a tenth of your spices – mint, dill and cumin. But you have neglected the more important matters of the law – justice, mercy and faithfulness.' Presumably Jesus was familiar with the words of the prophet Micah. It is in any case interesting that he gives a similar 'trinity' to Micah.
[71] Jeremiah 22:3.
[72] Grey (1997), p. 69.
[73] Stenström, ed. (1992), 169ff.
[74] Sölle (2001), p. 191.
[75] Walters and Portmess (2001), p. 97.
[76] Walters and Portmess (2001), pp. 178-180.
[77] Fox (1979), p. 13.
[78] Woodruff (1982), p. 119.
[79] Einarsson (2005), p. 7-8.
[80] Isaac of Syria (2001), p. 71.

81 Hildegard of Bingen (1997), p. 116.
82 From *Evans' Diary*, taken from Gilbert (1986).
83 Chittister (2003), p. 15. I have used Joan Chittister's formulation of the twelve steps. If you read the rule yourself you will find them expressed a little differently and often more harshly.
84 Mechthild of Magdeburg (1998), p. 225.
85 Uhlein (1983), p. 78.
86 Sölle (2001), p. 209, and chapter 12.
87 Chapters 12-14 in Sölle (2001). In 1 Peter 1:1 and 2:11 we read about how the Christians regarded themselves as strangers in the world.
88 See especially his book *Creation Spirituality* (1991), Chapter 1.
89 Woodruff (1982), p. 30.
90 Mechthild of Magdeburg (1998), p. 258.
91 Mechthild of Magdeburg (1998), p. 79.
92 Mechthild of Magdeburg (1998), p. 323.
93 Quoted in Lanzetta (2005), p. 11.
94 Mechthild of Magdeburg (1998), p. 43.

Wild Goose Publications is part of the Iona Community, which is:

- An ecumenical movement of men and women from different walks of life and different traditions in the Christian church
- Committed to the gospel of Jesus Christ, and to following where that leads, even into the unknown
- Engaged together, and with people of goodwill across the world, in acting, reflecting and praying for justice, peace and the integrity of creation
- Convinced that the inclusive community we seek must be embodied in the community we practise

Together with our staff, we are responsible for:

- Our islands residential centres of Iona Abbey, the MacLeod Centre on Iona, and Camas Adventure Centre on the Ross of Mull

and in Glasgow:

- The administration of the Community
- Our work with young people
- Our publishing house, Wild Goose Publications
- Our association in the revitalising of worship with the Wild Goose Resource Group

The Iona Community was founded in Glasgow in 1938 by George MacLeod, minister, visionary and prophetic witness for peace, in the context of the poverty and despair of the Depression. Its original task of rebuilding the monastic ruins of Iona Abbey became a sign of hopeful rebuilding of community in Scotland and beyond. Today, we are about 250 Members, mostly in Britain, and 1500 Associate Members, with 1400 Friends worldwide. Together and apart, 'we follow the light we have, and pray for more light'.

For information on the Iona Community contact:
The Iona Community, Fourth Floor, Savoy House, 140 Sauchiehall Street, Glasgow G2 3DH, UK. Phone: 0141 332 6343
e-mail: admin@iona.org.uk; web: www.iona.org.uk

For enquiries about visiting Iona, please contact:
Iona Abbey, Isle of Iona, Argyll PA76 6SN, UK. Phone: 01681 700404
e-mail: ionacomm@iona.org.uk

Wild Goose Publications, the publishing house of the Iona Community established in the Celtic Christian tradition of Saint Columba, produces books, CDs and digital downloads on:

- holistic spirituality
- social justice
- political and peace issues
- healing
- innovative approaches to worship
- song in worship, including the work of the Wild Goose Resource Group
- material for meditation and reflection

For more information, please contact us at:

Wild Goose Publications
Fourth Floor, Savoy House
140 Sauchiehall Street,
Glasgow G2 3DH, UK

Tel. +44 (0)141 332 6292
Fax +44 (0)141 332 1090
e-mail: admin@ionabooks.com

or visit our website at
www.ionabooks.com
for details of all our products and online sales